I dedicate this book to my daughter Kristi Lea Abramson

and to all the entrepreneurs throughout the world.

May this book serve as an invaluable tool to blaze your own pathway to success.

We live in amazing times.
There are more opportunities than ever before so DREAM BIG!

YOU CAN TOO

ERROL ABRAMSON

Contents

Introduction 18
LESS THAN HUMBLE BEGINNINGS 21
FIRST TASTE OF PRIDE 27
VALUABLE LESSON 31
MY WHOLE WORLD CHANGED 38
STARTING A NEW LIFE 47
GREYHOUND AND HERE I GO 57
STRUGGLING WITH MONEY 62
I AM GOING TO DRIVE A FERRARI 73
MR. HILL 81
MY FIRST TWO BUSINESS VENTURES 85
MY ROAD TO REAL ESTATE 103
BACK IN WINNIPEG 114
GET THE CASH 120
GOING NORTH TO GILLEM 131
WHAT OPPORTUNITIES COULD I FIND? ... 140
BACK IN OAHU, HAWAII 153
THE BIG SHIFT 158
MY NEW APARTMENT COMPLEX 168
UNISURF UNITED WE STAND 179
BACK IN HAWAII 192
HELLO BIG APPLE 197
BACK IN PEG! 221
ALOHA AGAIN! 255
OPTIONS 258

SAVE ME CANADIAN SUN 264
OFF TO THE CAYMAN ISLANDS 271
OMEGA MARKET LTD 288
THE RCMP ALWAYS GETS THEIR MAN 309
I AM A FARMER NOW 322
WELCOME TO THE HUDSON BAY 333
THE HUGE MISTAKES 345
ONE MORE ROUND WITH   THE
GOVERNMENT 353
THE HEALTH MAGAZINE WITH TEETH 357
TIME TO EXIT 364
MLM HERE I COME 378
OUT OF ADVERSITY, HELLO CHINA! 389
DREAM BIG 392

1990 was a very difficult year. I had experienced a huge financial loss in the housing industry and had lost my management position. I had a wife and three young children and no way to support them. I was down as low as anyone could get. I picked up pop cans at constructions sites for money to help the finances. A friend asked me to come and listen to this person speak. I had heard them all before. There was not a motivational trainer or wealth management coach that I had not heard. Anyway, I am glad that this friend dragged me to listen and meet Errol Abramson. There was something different about this guy. He had a swagger about himself that I liked. His stories made sense. The way he could make you laugh and cry all within the same story was incredible. More importantly was the story of his life. If Errol could make it and be a success anyone could, so I decided to listen. I decided to eat every word of the teaching. I began to retell the stories as if they were mine. I began to walk, talk and follow Errol Abramson until I became like him, and now I can say that after 24 years my life has changed.

Errol has been a tremendous success in business, and he knows how to do it and teach it. I think the most important goal for Errol is just to help people get the most out of life as he spends his time putting his effort into helping people grow from where they are now to where they want to be. My children have benefited from what I have learned from Errol, and now the 2nd generation is successful, each in their chosen careers. Errol does not play around with this. If you are serious and want to change then just follow what he says, as I did. For many years now I live the life that most only dream about. Thank you, Errol, for giving all this to me.

Lorence Irvine
CEO
Many Companies
Philippines

"When you have the one person you can absolutely trust with your heart and soul; your business, there really is no limit to what you want to achieve!"

I just want to thank Errol for the mentoring he provides to me, for my business and to anyone who is lucky enough to be a part of the Entrepreneur School mentoring Errol provides. Errol has opened the doors and my mind to now getting more than 100X ROI from what I had originally started with six months ago!

**Tyson Wong,
Digital Evaluation Media Ltd
Vic President
Facebook Ads For Authors & Experts
Burnaby BC Canada**

When it comes to pure business genius, Errol Abramson is one of a kind. His ability to identify blocks and deliver creative solutions is simply unparalleled. As an owner of multiple businesses, I have witnessed and benefited from Errol's gifts time and again. He is not just a gifted entrepreneur but also an excellent teacher whose biggest attribute is not just his track record but the size of his heart

**Peter Sage
CEO**

**Sage International
UK**

Errol has been an incredible mentor and role model to me for over 18 years. He has been an inspiration in helping me develop as an entrepreneur and encouraging me to follow my dreams. Errol has proven success across many industries and businesses with an incredible track record of wins not only benefiting himself but most important making a difference in the lives of tens of thousands of people worldwide. He has not only been an incredible entrepreneur, but Errol is one of the most entertaining and inspirational motivational speakers. Errol's life story is an inspiration for anyone that has the desire to learn the formula for success.

**Rob Baker
Founder/CEO
Empowerment Flex Marketing
Dallas TX**

I have always felt that the teacher is the most valuable asset in our society. I don't know where a lawyer or a politician became worth more than a teacher? It is sad where education has gone. In fact, that is the big question: where did it go?

For things to change, we must change, and for things to get better we must get better. That makes sense, so where has education gone? Today, most homes have both spouses working or single parents running the show. Has school become a government babysitter? How many can afford a private school? Then comes the curriculum. Big question! When a child graduates from high school are they equipped to take on real life, out there? Have we been taught real skills that will serve us well? Come on: NO!

If you are lucky, you are an above average athlete and your abilities open doors for you. If not, there's college, if you can afford it. Paths become defined at an early age. And who we hang with starts to define our behavior. We accept what we see and experience as "the way it is." We get a job, establish our social life, date, marry and have kids. In short, we learn to fit in. For those of us that move on to college maybe we get a better job and a middle-class lifestyle. We get by!!!!

Most of us don't even question our position in life. We learn to make excuses and justify where we are, who we are and why we got there. Some of us become pretty good at it, until we believe it.

If you think you can, or think you can't, you are right!!! The truth is not many people care either way. When you are miserable, 80% of the people could care less, and the other 20% are glad.

I was watching the World Cup and was deeply touched by the emotional expression of pride" people felt for their countries. I saw them crying, devastated at their counties loss, or elated at their victory. I was stirred by the PRIDE expressed in the singing of their national anthems.

Pride, I believe, is one of the most beautiful words in the English language. What do the books say about it?

"Feeling or deep pleasure or satisfaction derived from one's own achievements, the achievements of those with whom one is closely associated, or from qualities or possessions that are widely admired."

Pride is the dignified sense of what is due to oneself or self-respect; self-esteem. Pride is pleasure, joy, gratification, fulfillment, satisfaction and a sense of achievement. It is taking pride in a job well done with an inordinate self-esteem.

Now, honestly, when is the last time you felt that way? When is the last time you made your children (if you have any) feel that way?

Why do we find it easier to put people down then build them up? I can only speak from my experience. I will share with you my insight into this important feeling that we are not taught about in school, except in athletics.

We are subject to so many negative influences throughout our youth and into adulthood that all the things in which we would, could or should take pride is stripped away. So many of us are in a safe harbor, clinging on to what might be left of our self-esteem.

Why though can't or shouldn't you have anything and everything you desire, as long as you don't hurt others or break laws getting it?

What if I were to tell you that just a minor change in attitude could radically alter your life? I have witnessed it many times with people from all walks of life. They make the most unbelievable changes in their lives time and time again.

Errol's wisdom and patience have brought the best out of me. As a highly creative I can at times be so caught in the creation of a business that I don't get it done. Errol's concepts and teachings have caused me to grow my implementation skills and have made me confident that I can get results. Because of Errol's coaching, I gained the skills and confidence to not only get results for my own business but increase and impact the bottom line of others business. My experience with him has been life changing in my confidence, my finances and ability to lead others into success. When Errol coaches you, he goes beyond the average coach. He genuinely cares for your overall wellbeing, giving you solid results in your business and lasting change in your personal life. Errol has even touched my son's life. As a single mother and entrepreneur Errol Abramson has influenced my son and shifted my financial future.

Tia Ross
Co-creator of LegacyShifters.com
CEO of TiaRossandcompany.com
Founder of iseeyourgreatness.org
San Diego California USA

Introduction

Look, it is not the big things but the small ones that make a big difference. If a plane is taking off from London, Heathrow, heading for Capetown, South Africa, and it is just an inch off course, without correction, will it hit Capetown? Of course not! That's why there's an on-board computer to make course corrections and keep the plane on track. When you started out, you might have been off course an inch or two, and here you are, reading this book.

Let me illustrate a little better. During my lectures, I like to show the crowd what I mean about changing your thinking, just a little. The metaphor I enjoy is this.

I stand on the stage in front of the strongest retaining wall I can find, preferably something concrete.

I start to punch my hand and make a few karate moves like I am going to punch the wall. Then I announce that I am going through that wall. I ask the crowd how many you think I can do it? No one raises their hands. Then I ask how many think I can't do it? They all agree I can't.

I confirm I am going through, still punching my hand, and walk to the wall. Then, I stop and say: now, if I got a hammer how many think I can get through? What about a Jack Hammer? How about some C-4 explosive?

Now, how many think I am going through at that point: 100%.
Do you get it? In a matter of a minute, we turned what appeared impossible 180 degrees to the possible.

Is it that simple? You bet!!

I did it and "YOU CAN TOO!!

Errol Abramson is not only a stellar business coach but a caring friend who helped me with personal family challenges. I have had the honor to be mentored by one of the most brilliant minds who has successfully created over 47 successful businesses. More meaningful to me is his heart of giving and helping others. Errol knows how to ask the right questions to lead me to very solid decisions. He has helped me to focus and prioritize. I have been better able to look at problems in different ways, thus finding very meaningful solutions. And of course, his profit centers and green and red activity have laser the focus and Shifted the direction of my business.

Today Legacy Shifters has such an opportunity to leverage its growth by the multiple streams of income Errol has helped create for us. He has designed a 5-star SHIFT travel that supports the whole SHIFT movement. And the introduction to his wonder friends and partners now are giving us the opportunity to sell our SHIFT Coaching in Major Big Stores.

Kris Miller
Financial planner
Developer of personal living trusts
Author Motivational Speaker
Co-creator of LegacyShifters.com
Hemet California USA

LESS THAN HUMBLE BEGINNINGS

Born in Winnipeg Manitoba, in 1950, I can remember it was cold; the winters were so cold. My parents smartened up and moved to California in 1953. My mother, Shirley was one of four sisters, one of which, Betty, had already moved to California. We followed. My mother had suffered the loss of her parents. Her father, when I was one and her mother, to diabetes when I was three. I was too young to understand her grieving and how deeply it affected her. She was a loving mother but never got over her loss. She would tell me, "Arie" (my Hebrew name, Errol being the English), "I only have graves in Winnipeg." I didn't understand her pain, but it would become very clear in my later years. We lived in a one-bedroom apartment just outside of Santa Monica where my mother's sister Betty lived with her husband Ed and son Howard. Ed was a big man at 6'7", as was his brother Hank at 6'5", while Betty was a small woman of barely 5'3". Ed was a mechanic. He and his brother had a gas station with three bays in the back for car repairs. This is where I gained one of my first business influences. My father, Art, worked for them, pumping gas and doing odd repairs. I remember asking my dad why don't we get our own gas station? He looked at me like I was from outer space. On the weekends, we would go with Betty's family, the Baizers, to the beach. At Pacific Ocean Park (POP) there were three piers. Ed would surf fish, and I learned how to surf. I first body surfed then took up using a board. I was seven years old at the time and became passionate about the waves.

There were good surfing breaks around the pier, and I usually could get someone to lend me a board. This passion lead me to my first entrepreneurial endeavor. I went to Chuck Dent Surfboards, in Huntington Beach, with an older boy who had bought from him. The board I wanted to be made was 10' long and very colorful. It was going to cost 100 bucks. I needed 50% down and a 4-week lead time.

I washed cars, mowed lawns, babysat, delivered newspapers, and walked dogs to get the down payment. I was so proud when I order the board. When the salesman asked how old I was, I replied: how old do you have to be to buy a surfboard? He just wrote up the receipt.

During that time, we had moved to a house in La Puente, California. about 30 miles away from Betty. My dad got a deal on a house. What a neighborhood! We bordered on a stockyard, and when the wind was at us, you needed a close pin on your nose. We were 20 miles from the beach. I worked hard and had the balance for the board and was ready to take delivery. My dad agreed to drive me with a friend supplying board racks and some paraffin wax as a gift.

When we got to the shop I was so excited I almost peed my pants. The board was on the rack in the front of the shop, and it was beautiful. It had three-burgundy strips with yellow in between. I pulled out my fifty to pay then looked down at the invoice. It was $104. TAX!!! I didn't have the four bucks. I was devastated. My friend had .85, and I had .60. My Dad put up the four dollars. We loaded my new baby in the car and headed home. I was melting the wax to put a hot wax coat on the deck. I was taking it out the next day.

23

There I was, in our front yard, proudly waxing up my new board, with neighbors dropping by for a look and I overheard my dad telling a guy he bought it for me. Later that night I asked my dad why he said that. Wasn't he proud of me for earning the money for the board? He said if he had not given me the four dollars, could I have bought the board? I didn't understand, but I guessed he was right, as I didn't have the four dollars. We as parents can really affect our kid's self-esteem.

My dad wasn't a very nice guy. He took a lot of credit for my accomplishments. Like, little league. I was an exceptional athlete. I was the best hitter in the league and a very strong pitcher. My dad told everyone he trained me. We had played catch a few times, but that was it. He just wasn't a good dad. He was from a family of four brothers and one sister. I never got really close to any of them, except my Uncle Chuck. Chuck was the baby brother of my dad's family. He was the successful one. He owned a cab company and had many other interests. He was my first real mentor before I even knew what that meant. I never knew my grandparents on my dad's side, either. They were both gone before I was born. My dad was a tough guy as was his brother Chuck. Dad's solution for everything was hitting. Mom was a gentle soul and just not a happy person. She wanted me to have advantages, but money was always an issue. Her sisters had husbands in business, and she felt my dad should have a business as well. He was a lazy sort and much preferred to complain how unfair the world was and that it owed him a living.

I first started coaching with Errol in November 2015. I was a young and relatively inexperienced CEO who had become responsible for a small family business after my father retired. Scared that I would make a critical mistake that would endanger the business or destroy it, I reached out for some professional help. Contacting Errol was my lucky break, here was a retired CEO who, over his life, had run multiple businesses of all scales, from tiny single operator businesses to multi-billion national retail chains. A no-nonsense, take no prisoners and accept no excuses, get sh*t done... The absolute master of productivity and business. The first thing he told me was to relax, because with him *in my corner, there was just no way the business would fail. I have been working with Errol for over a year now, and in that year, I have grown my business significantly, rebranded it, taken on larger offices, more employees, seen my revenue increase and my profits grow. All I can say is if you need some help, or are looking for a business coach, there is literally, no one else with the level of experience or expertise as Errol. Couldn't recommend him highly enough and looking forward to working with him for years to come.*

Oscar Scheiner
Chief Executive Officer
www.bensnaturalhealth.com
UK

FIRST TASTE OF PRIDE

My dad got a job driving an 18-wheeler, delivering milk for Golden Cream Farms. He was a teamster and being in the union suited him just fine. He would get up at 4 AM, as they delivered to supermarkets before opening. I loved going to work with him as he worked Saturdays and had Tuesday's and Sunday's off. We'd drive in the big rig and dad would back into these tight loading docks. I guess all kids want to be proud of their dad, and so I was watching him work. All the guys knew him and shouted his name on the dock. I would help unload; then the guys would go for coffee. I would have this big bagel, loaded with cream cheese.

Mom still struggled emotionally with losing her parents. It was something she would never get over. She was having mental issues and was under a doctor's care. Two times we went back to Winnipeg for her to get treatment. I didn't understand that she was spending time in mental hospitals; no one ever explained this to me. In fact, they covered it up, saying she was just in the hospital. Both times my uncle Chuck paid for our trip up and the treatment. My dad's insurance did not cover mental illness unless it was job-related.

Mom wouldn't fly, so twice we took the train. Uncle Chuck arranged for a private sleeper car, and all the meals were included. They would bring cookies and small cakes to our room. This was first class, or so I thought.

Chuck would meet us at the station, and he was very kind to Mom and I. He drove us to my Aunt Thelma's house, on Inkster Boulevard, in the North End of Winnipeg. I lived with them while mom underwent treatment. The living room couch was my bed. I had two cousins. Arie had the same name as me in Hebrew, but his English name was Earl and mine was Errol. Our other cousins called me "more Arie." Well, it was "little Arie," but I outgrew him so "more Arie" covered it. Then there was my cousin Sheila. She was the most loving person in my life. She was like a big sister. She was the only one that would try to explain what was wrong with my mom. Their family owned a bakery, City Bread.

Theirs was the best rye bread in the country. They had a three-bedroom, one bath, two-story house. My uncle came down the stairs at 3 am each morning to go open the bakery. Daily, they shipped their rye bread across Canada. Some days I would get up with him, and he'd invite me to work. Oh, this was great. To this day I can smell the fresh bread baking in the warehouse ovens that rotated it as it baked. The staff would be so busy, rushing about. Several airline containers sat by the loading dock, waiting for the fresh baked rye. Within an hour they were filled, picked up and gone.

There was the retail shop in front. On the days I went in with my Uncle, Aunty Thelma would come in later, for her shift. I would come forward and help bagging the bread, helping old ladies to the door. It was fun. Again, I felt pride in my family. They made pastries which I would eat while they were cooling, nothing tastes better than these freshly baked delights. At nine years old, this was the closest I could come to being left alone in a candy store, instructed to eat all I wanted.

Thelma was a wonderful, loving woman. She later became my golf buddy, but for now, she was caring for her sick sister's son. My mom finished her treatment, and we returned to La Puente.

VALUABLE LESSON

My home life was tough. My dad injured his back in a work-related accident. He got a nice claim and didn't work for a while. I never saw any evidence of his injury at home. His claim was that his back was screwed up, and he couldn't lift much, anymore. This left him unable to do his job.

Mom started to get worse and constantly in and out of institutions. I had to miss a good deal of school to care for my brother and help mom when she was home.

In school, I found it very hard to read. There wasn't much information on dyslexia in 1963. It was embarrassing for me to read out loud in class. I thought I was dumb. I had a great memory, so if teachers would review for tests and give the answers, I would score well. Take spelling for instance. The teacher provided a list of words to learn each week. When the Friday test came around, I would score 100%.

When I was in 7th grade, my IQ was tested twice. The first time was just before a football game. All I wanted to do was get out to the field, so I made nice patterns on the multiple-choice test sheet.

In those days we graded our own tests to save time, so I was given the answers. Well, I scored very low. My score was so low in fact that I was retested. Now, remember, I had a strong memory and had seen the answers. It was such a long test that they never considered that previously seeing the answers could be a factor.

My IQ was over 170, so was I a genius or an idiot? When they assessed my schoolwork, I was a B student and a good athlete. I have moved up a grade and put in a gifted student experimental program. These kids were smart. Several of them were also athletes. I formed my first "mastermind" years before I would learn what that was. I felt I was out of place, as I knew I had trouble reading. The embarrassment caused me to hide that fact as best as I could.

In late in my sophomore year, I had to accompany mom to Winnipeg, again. She was hospitalized, and I was forced to enroll in school there. Classroom protocol was much more disciplined than that in California. The teacher carried around a yardstick, and she would slap students she felt were out of line. One day, about three weeks into my attendance, I was asking another student about an assignment I didn't hear. She came from behind me and whacked my left hand, placed on the desktop, excessively hard. I grabbed the yardstick from her and slapped her hand with it. "How do you like it," I said, as she let out a painful yell. Then I stood up and broke the yardstick in half to the joyful students' approval.

That landed me in the head master's office. My aunt was summoned. My defense was the teacher had not written the assignment on the blackboard. I was inquiring for clarification, as a good student should when I was assaulted with excessive force. I simply defended myself; she should be charged with abuse and suspended.

There was a suspension all right: me!!!! AND THEY DIDN'T WANT ME BACK! My aunt was none too happy with me. Today, a teacher could never do that. I was just ahead of my time.

Mom was released from the hospital, and we returned to California. I was happy to be back. I surfed a lot that summer and resumed my baseball with the Pony League. It was a great summer. I had a part-time job at a hardware store and lumberyard, with one of the players on my football team. I worked hard and even came up with some security procedures. Previously, customers would order lumber to be cut, after driving back to have it loaded, some drove away without paying. There was no record kept, so the company never knew.

My idea was to have a three-part order book in the back. We'd cost it out, write up the order, then send the customer to the front with two copies. When they returned with the two copies marked paid, then we would load them up taking one copy and stapling it into the order book. They adopted my concept with little thanks and no pay increase. Later, I was let go when business slowed down. It was because I had the least seniority, they said. It was a valuable lesson for my later business life.

By my junior year, I was a starter again on the varsity football team. This makes you popular on campus. The guys I hung out with were other football players and surfers. What a dichotomy, but it worked for me. My football friends were tough guys always getting into fights. My surfer mates were passive with life, though aggressive with waves. Home life remained tough. Dad was drinking more. Money was scarce. He had blown through his settlement and taken a security job at the Mattel toys plant. He worked a rotation shift two weeks on days, then afternoons, then the graveyard. He even carried a gun, though it was optional. I never knew what he was paid for any of his jobs. I was very naïve about a lot of things in life. I had no real training at the family level. I would see other relatives having their own businesses, but dad said they were stupid, taking all that risk when he got a paycheck every two weeks with great benefits. I guess we were the lower middle class at the time. The guys I hung with, for the most part, were the same. I was also behind the curve on girls. Oh, they liked me, but I didn't know how to respond. The guys would tell stories, and I would just try to look like I knew what they were talking about. I didn't. I was more Sir Richard Branson's brand…….! Get it?

The football season was great for me. I started as a guard, but they converted me to inside linebacker. I got a lot of satisfaction out of the move. It was a way for me to contribute more and I must say I loved the hitting.

Mom went into an institution again. We never spoke about any of this at home. If I were to ask my dad, he would not answer or tell me it was not my business. Funny that no one ever spoke to the children. My brother was a cool kid. I would let him hang with me. Take him to the beach or football practice. He wasn't interested in playing sports but enjoyed being a fan. The other guys and even the coaches treated him well. It was hard for him, with a mom that was unavailable and a father that just didn't care. There was a lot of pressure on me to raise him. I didn't mind; he was my brother, I loved him.

I am not sure how that relationship affected him or me. We just got by. Looking back, I just didn't get to be a kid myself. I had to grow up so fast, and sadly that was going to get worse.

MY WHOLE WORLD CHANGED

I was a year ahead in school so, now, I am just turning fourteen. My brother Hersh is turning nine. We are both May babies: him the 6th and me the 30th. I am a big kid, so my age doesn't affect the way people see me. Plus, I am an athletic star, so my life on the outside looked good.

Toward the end of the school year, something blew me away: scholarship offers from major colleges. I wasn't even sure what it meant, but other people were impressed, so it must be good. College was the topic on almost all the students' minds. Most of my friends were thinking about a junior college. My dad made sure to point out the expense. His opinion was it was unnecessary and a waste of time and money.

Mom was getting worse now. She was continually in and out of the hospital. I was again missing school to care for her. Some days she wouldn't get out of bed. Dad seemed to pretend that nothing was wrong. Hersh was in school all day. He would get home before me and play at a neighbor's until I got back from school. Dad was on afternoon shifts that week, so if mom cooked dinner, we all ate. If not, I took care of Hersh.

It seemed to be a good morning. Mom was up and making breakfast; she seemed happy. I remember Hersh ate cereal and she made me my favorite, fried banana sandwiches. You toast bread, butter both sides, and put them in a hot frying pan, then flip them and add the bananas. Once put together, wow, they were yummy!!! This day she made me two. I ate one on the spot and the other on my way to the bus. Mom gave both Hersh and I a huge hug and kiss.

It was a normal day at school. I did not play baseball that year for the school; the same jerk was coaching. It's sad, as I was a better baseball player than football. It was my last year of Pony League, and I was leading the league in home runs. One of our baseball players was given a scholarship to USC. He was a very strong left-handed pitcher. He threw hard. I actually liked batting against him. I was a switch hitter and took him on from the right side of the plate. We didn't like each other much, either. His brother played for my team. He was a very talented shortstop. I had parked two on this pitcher this year. He had a huge ego, and it was nice to take the slow jog around the bases on him. He had fanned me more than once, as well. He would have his brother tell me that those were his best strikeouts of the season. I rebutted, too bad they never beat us.

That afternoon I took the bus home. I didn't have a clue what I would find. The house was quiet. Hersh must have been on the street playing, and I thought my mom was sleeping, but her bedroom door was open. I looked in the room. The bed was made, so I called to her with no answer. She would, from time to time, visit with the neighbors, so I thought nothing of it. I called one of my surfer friends that lived up the street. We were organizing a trip down south as a nice swell was running. He suggested I come over and see his new board. I agreed and went into the garage to get my bike. The door from the house into the garage was through my parents' room.

I cannot express what I saw or how I felt. It just cut right through my soul. My mom had hung herself. I screamed, "Oh my God." I could see from her color she was long gone. I rushed to the phone and called 911, then my dad's work. The fire engines arrived first, sirens blazing. They rushed in with life support equipment. The police arrive about 5 minutes later. The firemen came back out and spoke to the police. Neighbors were at the door, and I just blurted out what I had seen. I was in shock but didn't know it. One of the neighbor ladies was trying to hold me. I was just repeating, where is Hersh, please don't let him come home. I didn't realize I was screaming until a policeman grabbed me. They put a lock on the outside of the garage and yellow tape, as my Dad pulled up. He had to park in the street as the fire engine was in the driveway. He came into the house, and one of the policemen escorted him into the garage. He was out two minutes later with tears in his eyes.

We spent two hours in the house; then detectives arrived to investigate. Dad and I were questioned. They let me go to see my brother. The neighbor said she would keep him for dinner, and not to worry. I didn't say anything to him. He was in the backyard, and I guess they told him there was a little fire in our garage. I called my surfer friend, and he said his parents asked if I wanted to spend the night. I didn't know at the time what anyone had asked me. Hersh was on my mind. My dad didn't ask me if I was okay or anything about Hersh. It just seemed to be all about him. Okay, he had lost his wife. In fact, no professional ever spoke to me, until I sought help, many years later.

The police stayed for hours and then the medical examiner came and did tests. My dad was busy getting sympathy from all the neighbors. I asked him if I could bring Hersh home to give him the news. He told me he just couldn't deal with it now. He left it to me. Wow, really!!! So I went down the street and collected my brother. I made him a little dinner and then told him that mom was in heaven.

A neighbor suggested Hersh stay with her and that she would get him off to school with her son. I wanted desperately to be out of that house and felt it best for my brother as well. Dad was across the street and well into a bottle of something with some well-meaning neighbors. I told him were Hersh was and informed him that I was going to a friend's house as well.

It was well after 10 pm when my friend picked me up. The garage was still locked with yellow tape, and the door from inside the house was taped. He pulled in and saw it, but didn't comment.

My friend was two years ahead of me, so he was in college. Our bond was surfing and music. His dad owned a music store. His younger brother was an accomplished guitar player. I had many dinners at their house and stayed over so we could leave early for the waves. They were a real family. We would all dine together with interesting talks. It was always a joy to spend time with them. His dad would sit at the piano and start a sing-along. His brother would get the guitar out, and we'd all join in.

That night there was no singing. He had told his parents what had transpired and they were all up waiting for us to arrive. His mother held me so tight. We never said a word. I was set up in his room as usual. We were going to surf in the morning. It was Thursday, and I would miss school. I couldn't get my board out of my garage, so I would ride his old one. They were an upscale family with a nice house on a large lot with a pool. Other friends had pools, but this was by far the nicest home I had ever stepped foot in.

It was impossible to sleep. I laid awake until his alarm went off. It was still dark, and we were 45 minutes from his favorite break. The first song on the radio was "Ruby Tuesday," by the Stones. To this day, I can't listen to it: it transports me back to that day.

He dropped me off at around 5 pm. Dad was smoking in the living room. He hadn't picked up my brother. He informed me that we were going to Betty's house on Saturday. Later, I found out that my mom's sister, Betty, and her family, paid all the funeral expenses. This wasn't the first time my dad had sidestepped our obligations, nor was it the last. I had pride and wanted to pay our own way. The truth is I didn't know how poor we were or how my dad squandered our money. These lessons would also come later.

Friday, I attended school. What a day. The kids at the bus stop said nothing even though everyone knew. On the bus, there were kids seated, as we were the second of three stops. There were two girls that liked me. They had invited me over to study and parties, but I never accepted. They were both nice, and I did consider them friends. At the sight of me, one jumped up out of her seat, saying "Oh Errol," and hugged me as she started crying. The other joined in, and the three of us sat in the two-seat row as they held me. I was consoling them as we drove to school.

At school, the athletes rallied around me. I wasn't prepared for – nor did I want – sympathy. The football coaches also were very attentive. The new head coach of the football team suggested I work out, thinking it might help me. I did; it didn't.

I was becoming numb. I honestly didn't know what I was feeling. By the time we had the funeral I was feeling nothing. The friend I spent the night with was a pallbearer, and his family attended. The football coaches also were there. I was in a daze. All I remember was my dad collecting as much sympathy as he could get. I said nothing that day.

STARTING A NEW LIFE

School ended with me attending the football camp for next year's team. My dad informed me that we would be vacationing in Winnipeg this summer and it was non-negotiable. He also failed to inform me that he had sold the house until just before we were to leave. I packed off my surfing equipment to a friend in the neighborhood. I'd left a lot of stuff behind as we loaded into dad's station wagon. Off went the three of us to Canada. I was bitter about the trip. Summers in California were fun. I would surf almost every day. Hang out with either surfer or football friends. The two groups were very opposite, and I learned there was a different protocol with each. Although I did have one friend from the football side that surfed. He still didn't like to hang with my surfer group. He called them potheads, which, for the most part, was true. Now, he and many of the other guys did smoke pot, but only my surfer group won that title. I wasn't much into drugs. Maybe it was my mom's influence I am not sure. Oh, sure I tried everything, but the feeling of being out of control bothered me. I just never got the benefit of the experience.

I would miss that summer. Here we were in Winnipeg. My Aunt Thelma had arranged for a rental across the street from her house. It was a one bedroom with three single beds in that one bedroom. It was very simple, but it worked. Dad took a job driving a cab for his brother. Uncle Chuck had a farm called the Triple R. The Rat Race Retreat was located outside the city. He was my first real influence. This was a great place. It was a large plot of land running from the main street to the waterfront on the Red River. His house sat on the front of the property with two large fenced pastures. There was a road to the barn with six horses, a riding area, and a boathouse. There was also a dock with a large yacht and a floatplane moored to it. This was some place, and one guy owned it all, my uncle! Above the boathouse was an office, which my uncle and his cronies frequented to drink beer and bullshit. These all were successful men with businesses in Winnipeg. Chuck gave me a job mucking the stalls and tending to the horses. I took to it like therapy. I spent the weekends there, only returning home to sleep. He taught me how to ride and care for the horses. He was like a real dad. I hadn't realized how hungry I was for that bond.

This was the first time I was this close to success. Chuck seemed to be someone that had everything. I went to his cab company office and garage, where he again employed me, this time to wash the cabs. He would always pay me in cash and, oh my god; he would pull out a wad of hundreds neatly folded with a money clip. This is the way I carry my money to this day, wrapped around my credit cards in my front left pocket.

My dad would take me to work, and I would wash and clean his cab for his shift. I asked him why he didn't buy a few cabs and start our family business. He never answered me. One of Chuck's friends owned a lumberyard, Portage Lumber. It was owned by brothers. One had an estate just up the road from Chuck. He wanted to clean the grounds and one day when they were drinking Chuck yelled down for me to join them. He always asked me if I wanted a beer, but I knew it was a test and refused. He always complimented me on that and would open a pop. He said he had a job for me. It wasn't a choice or a question. It was an order. I knew better than to cross him after they had been a few hours into their drinking. He was a tremendously flawed man but with a huge loving heart for his family, which he would not allow himself to show often. I was so impressed with his material success that I never focused on anything else. Well, he negotiated the terms of my employment. The next day, he drove me up to his friend's farm. It was a big job, clearing and trimming. I was given some simple instructions. Chuck thought the job would take the balance of the summer. I didn't mind hard work, and I was left alone to guide myself. I worked until sunset and was back the next morning at first light. At 8 am the friend came out of his house, which was much grander than my uncles. He surveyed my work and complimented me on my efforts. Little did he know that I would finish the job that day. Chuck stopped by to see how I was getting along with a corn beef sandwich and a coke. He called me Arie, my

Hebrew name, which most of the family did. Errol was used in California, but I liked Arie.

That night the grounds were neat and clean of all the mess. The next morning the friend, Lenard, had his truck and a couple of men cart off the piles of waste. Lenard was amazed at my hard work and landscaping creativity. He had called Chuck, who showed up as the last load was removed, while I cleaned up each area. The two men were having coffee in front of the house when I arrived. Chuck put five crisp one hundred dollar bills in my hand. I didn't even know what my pay was and the only other time I had seen a hundred-dollar bill was when Chuck pulled out his billfold. Wow! I tried to conceal my excitement, but it was evident to all. I was offered a job at his lumberyard, starting tomorrow. I accepted and stashed the bills in my pocket and headed for the bus stop.

I showed my aunt my huge score. She thought it was a lot of money to pay a boy for two days work. She didn't see the work I had done, only the time I had put in. My

51

dad was a different story. He saw it as an opportunity to grab some. He suggested I put three hundred to the rent since he was short this month. Then Hersh needed new shoes and school clothes. Why did he need school clothes if we are here on vacation, I asked?

"Listen," Dad explained, "I sold everything in California; we are home here in Winnipeg, now. I want you to go down to the school and see about enrolling," he continued. This was a shock to me. I did not want to live here; my life was in California. I did go down to the school. It was a disaster. First, they felt I had to go back the grade I had skipped. Second, and even more devastating, there were no sports programs. Not even a physical education class. All sporting activities were done through the community service clubs. Each sport had their own organizers. To be fair, I visited two, baseball and football, which was Canadian style, with three downs. Both were weak at best. At the football camp, you had to supply your own equipment. Many of the boys had a different helmet, some had shoulder pads, and none had proper football pants with thigh protection. I threw the ball around with the guys all nice enough. The highlight of their season was that they got to go meet the professional team the, "Winnipeg Blue Bombers."

My dad had no sympathy for my situation at all. We finally had it out, which was not pleasant, ending in the last slap to the face he ever gave me. I let him know in no uncertain terms that I would retaliate if he ever again raised a hand to my brother or me.

I asked why we couldn't be in business, like all our other relatives. Why did he have to drive a cab for his brother, why not drive his own. I admit I said things I shouldn't have. I wanted more for him, my brother and me. He was enjoying though the sympathy the family gave him, along with the handouts. Honestly, that made me sick.

I missed my friends and the ocean. Most of all I missed my mom, which was an area we never discussed. At best, I was confused. Why was this happening to me? I bet we can all recall a situation in which we felt hopeless. Also, I loved my brother, and the thought of leaving him with dad pushed me to stay. I took the job at the lumberyard. I was half expecting my dad to pay me back the rent money, along with all the money I spent on my brother's clothes and school supplies. It never happened. I continued to work weekends on my uncle's farm. He gave me 20 dollars a weekend. He was proud of me and even started calling me son. I would bring Hersh out sometimes and give him rides on the horses. My aunty and her daughter Shelia became his real caregivers. My dad was just fine with that. The less responsibility he had to shoulder the better it suited him.

Finally, I realized it was going to be up to me. I made a plan to return to California. I called my coaches and explained my situation. I contacted some of my surfer friends. My aunt Betty and her husband Ed agreed to meet me and help me get started down there. They were wonderful people and always helpful, but I felt in my heart that it was sympathy and charity. At that time, just turning fifteen, I needed their help. They never complained and were rock solid throughout my entire life. The same can be said for all my mother's sisters and their families. If there was any love in my heart, it was for my brother and all of them. They taught me what family meant.

As an entrepreneur, Errol's success puts him in the top 1% of the top 1%. As a mentor, he has a unique ability to see the excuses I have been blind to. And of course, I can either live with the excuses or get the results I want, but not both. Two primary lessons Errol reinforces. And the more I live by these, the more I achieve. First, nothing happens until something is sold.

And second everything you do is either productivity (makes money) or activity (doesn't directly make money), so each day MUST start with productivity. Live by these and all you can do is be successful in business.

It's when I find (or tolerate) excuses to not do this, that I hit problems. Errol is a no-nonsense guy who kicks butt with a huge heart. His greatest reward is seeing my success. He has supported me. He has mentored me. He has pushed me. His successes are incredibly rare. His insights have come from achieving at a level most can barely get their head around. If all he did was share his knowledge and his insights that would be an incredible gift to any entrepreneur. But he not only shares, he genuinely cares. That combination makes him an incredible human being and makes me incredibly blessed.

Thank you, Errol.

Paul Elliott
Businessman and Motivational Speaker

GREYHOUND AND HERE I GO

My plan to return to California was taking shape. I had lodging through the coaches at a football team supporter's house. Their son was also on the team. I did inquire as to the costs, but they were all handled. One of my surfer friends, the same age and with better ability in the water, was now living at the beach. His parents spoiled him rotten. He would piss off other surfers with his smart mouth and bratty behavior, doing things like taking off in front of a surfer with a better position in the wave. I always bailed him out. He relied on me to save his ass just about every time we were in the water. His parents liked that, and I was included in many of the family outings.

His talent also gave him inroads with major surfing manufacturers: many sponsored him. I was good, though not in his league, we said we were cousins, and I was given sponsorship and club entries with him. We often traveled together, and until I broke from surfing, he was my best friend.

I had saved $384 for the summer. When I informed my dad of my departure date, he said he was planning on giving me back the money I had lent him, but now he would not support such a foolish idea. Like he had ever planned on repaying me.

My Uncle Chuck did try to get me to stay and keep the family together, but he understood and respected my decision. He asked what I had earned for the summer and how much I had to fund myself. I told him, and he matched it saying I had made him very proud, not only with his friends but the job I did for him on the farm. I had learned about and cared for his horse, which he said would miss me. I grew up a lot that summer and was ready for the challenge that laid ahead.

My cousin Shelia also supported me and said Hersh would be fine. She is such a beautiful person. She wanted to give me money, but I refused.

My bus ticket was $48 one-way to California. I had a green card, as we never turned them in when we came back to

Canada. My aunt Betty showed me how to renew, and I used their address. I spent my last two days with my brother, making sure he had everything he needed. Otherwise, we just played.

My dad drove me to the bus station. Once there, he promised me that if I got on that bus, he would not send a dime to help me out. A promise he kept, in fact, the worst. Our mother had social security benefits that were due my brother and I. It was $43 each a month. Dad had claimed them and was keeping them for himself. That money would have changed a great deal for me. I only found out later from a friend whose father had passed about the benefits he received. He showed me how to qualify. That was about two years after I was back in California. At that time, I went back to Winnipeg several times, but dad failed to mention those benefits. Social Security contacted me and informed me I was receiving the check in Canada, at my dad's address. My rent was 40 bucks a month that would have helped.

On that initial ride back to California, I was scared and excited at the same time. The bus ride was interesting. Six days in total: three days to Vancouver and three more to Santa Monica. My uncle Ed picked me up at the station. I had a surfboard at their house. I couldn't wait to get into the water. I spent the weekend with them. Aunty Betty loved the sun, Ed loved fishing, and me surfing. We would go to the beach a one-stop shop for all our needs. We would start with the set-up. Betty's stuff first, chair, towel, sun bag, plus the fully stocked cooler. Betty didn't come to the beach empty handed, oh no! There was plenty of food and drinks. There were times I thought she was setting up a concession stand. Then Ed's fishing gear, several polls, tackle box and a sand sifter to catch soft shell crabs for bait. He always set a pole for me. Before surfing, I would catch the crabs for the bait. Then my second job was to keep the surfers away from his lines, which many times would result in a fight. It was cool. I would normally win, and he would fish unencumbered by surfers. I wasn't a local at this break, but since I was a better surfer than the guys in the water, and I guess the fact that I beat the shit out of some of them, they let me be. These were great times and Ed and I would fish together for years. He and Betty watched my development over all these years.

Betty and all the sisters are gone now. They all had great influence in my life. My surfer friends picked me up, and we went and surfed Malibu, which had a great point break. If Brad came along, he was the best surfer in the water, and there were some very talented riders at this break. He would again piss off the locals, and I would step in. The guys liked having him along, as his mom would always fill the gas tank. But he could be a pain in the ass, too. He was just used to getting his way, and when the boys resisted, well, poop hit the fan. He would look to me for support, but with our crew, he was on his own and had a big slice of humble pie.

STRUGGLING WITH MONEY

My part-time job at a fast food joint gave me some lunch and weekend spending money. We would be at the events, and Brad's dad would sit on the beach and analyze the day's surf, planning a strategy for Brad to use during his upcoming heat. I knew his dad didn't know about the waves, but they spent that time together. It was strange to me, yet I envied it.

One event was way up North in Santa Cruz, "Steamers Lane." I was not rated high enough to enter. We went up the day before to surf the break. It was big! I liked big waves. In fact, the only time I ever beat Brad in a competition was in big waves. In small waves he was king. I had 20 dollars, and his dad asked to borrow it until we got home. This was the first I knew of their money problems. Of course, I gave it to him and said it was my contribution to the trip.

About two weeks later he sat me down and said if my dad couldn't send some support money he would have to send me back to Canada. Yikes!!!! There was no way my dad was sending anything. There was a group of surfers all from New York, Long Beach that lived across the street on the beach. When I asked them, they agreed to let me stay a few days on their couch. I spent another night in a car. Then, I found my home for the rest of the year: a lean-to shack, across from the Newport Beach pier. My rent was 40 bucks a month. It was a dump, but it was all mine. I had a double bed for sleeping and a single bed as a couch. The bathroom had a toilet and a tub with legs. You had to run the water to get the rust out of the pipes before you bathed. There were a small fridge and stove. The landlady let me store my boards in her garage after I gave one to her son. He sucked at surfing but had fun. It was my first PR job.

This became the spot to hang. These guys would be living in 10,000 square foot mansions, and they wanted to hang at my place. Well, there were no parents!!!

I was still embarrassed about my life and suffered from low self-esteem. School was fine, but I couldn't play sports as I transferred in the middle of the football season and there were rules about that. When baseball season rolled around, I wanted to play. I was in super shape and ready to go. Again, I ran into a coach that got in my way. This guy played favorites. It seemed the rich guys got priority with him.

The other coach was a nice guy and saw my talent, especially with the bat. They had a beautiful fenced field which I pounded balls out of from both sides of the plate. This coach said they could get me eligibility if the head coach applied.

The head coach's favorite was one of the richest kids in the school. He drove a Porsche 911S, wore designer everything, and lived on an estate in the hills. I went to a party at his home once. Wow! What a place. His dad was a junk bond trader. This was a lifestyle I had never experienced. I admit I was impressed, very impressed. He had one of the most beautiful girlfriends on campus. There will be a story about that later.

He had an ego and had been to my shack a few times with the boys. Make no mistake; he was one of them. He used to joke and call me ghetto boy. I let it slide, but it did hurt.

He would get out of long runs, doing special jobs for the coach, when we were sent off. I observed that this was a consistent pattern. I didn't help my case with the coach by confronting over the favoritism. Further, doubly stupid, I confronted him in front of other people. Add, to add to the tension; this kid was a pitcher. He was not bad, either, but I had his number and hit him hard. I had parked four and never struck out. I was on the second team, and we often played in pre-season.

I didn't make the team. The coach decided I was a troublemaker, with a bad attitude. So, he did not apply for my eligibility. There was some tension over this with the coaching staff and many of the players. I was clearly the best hitter on the team and a top defensive third baseman with a cannon for an arm. I provided strong relief pitching, too. The coach that liked me said it was a shame. I did go directly to the head coach, but he didn't acknowledge my protests.

I had a job at a Balboa restaurant. This was upscale. Their two signature dishes were live Atlantic lobster (flown in daily) and beef tenderloin medallions with Bernaise sauce. They charged $25 per lobster, and this was 1965. I had worked there as a dishwasher and now was a busboy. This was a big move as the waitresses were all women. (The owner only had sexy ladies working for him) I liked his style with that. The owner was a drunk. He was a tall, slender, gray-haired man, late 40's early 50's. He could get nasty with the staff and was a bit of a bully with the girls. He had sent a few off the floor crying. The later in the evening it got, the more vigilantly you watched out for him. He was over-nice to the clients. You know, the buttery smooth, kiss up type, and this crowd loved that special treatment. He once yelled at me for something stupid, and one of the girls put her hand on my back and took me away. I was learning about the importance of people skills.

The ladies gave a percentage of their tips to us busboys if we were attentive to the customers and helped with the heavy trays. I learned what they wanted: fill water, watch butter, clear plates, and pour coffee. I got on good with them all and was rewarded with cash. This became lunch money for school and an occasional movie. My paycheck went for rent food and clothes. Not much left over for no real savings. The chef liked me. He would slip me steaks for dinner. He was a cool guy, but it was his kitchen, and you didn't mess with anything. I had no idea what chefs made but heard the girls talk about how the owner got him here. On Friday and Saturday night I would help park cars during the busy times and make more tips. Then, late at night, when the bar was busy, and the restaurant traffic was done, I took over the lot for the regular guy so he could go home. He had a family and was a good guy, so I didn't mind. Plus, the last folks out were, for the most part, good tippers.

There was this one older lady. You could see she was beautiful in her younger days. She was a regular. She would usually meet people for dinner then retire to the lounge to listen to the three-piece jazz band. There she would slip into her Martini's and a drunken state. The first time I met her the owner had called me in. She was the last person in the bar. He handed me her car keys and instructed me to drive her home. He gave me directions to Lido Island, which I knew well. A few of my girlfriends lived there. This was more than upscale territory. You had to be rich to be in one of these properties. He and I helped her to the car. I got in the driver's seat. Oh, by the way, I was fifteen and didn't have a license. Well, no one ever asked!! I knew how to drive, and this was a Cadillac Eldorado. I parked in the driveway and helped her to the door. Her housekeeper opened the door and took her from me. Wait, she said. She went into her purse and pulled out a bill. I stuffed it in my pocket and thanked her as the door was closed. I walked home about a mile and a half. There were no cars to hitchhike that late. I got home and went right to bed. In the morning, emptying my pockets of my tip money, I found a one-hundred-dollar bill. I knew it had to be hers. My big dilemma, do I just keep it, as she did give it to me, or give it back. Surely someone would miss a hundred-dollar bill. I could be accused of stealing and lose my job. I walked back to her house. It looked even nicer in the daylight. I knocked, and the same lady answered, so I told her my story. I was shown to the pool area where the lady sat in a bathing suit. She smiled and greeted me. I pulled out the hundred and showed her saying, "You thought it was a dollar." and gave it to her. She looked down and smiled then walked into the house leaving me standing there. She returned with another hundred and said, "Honesty should be rewarded." Then she kissed me. The walk home seemed shorter. This became a ritual now when she came in she would find me and give me her car keys. The waitress got a good laugh out of it. They called her my sugar Momma. I just took the money.

I was dating a nice girl, also on Lido Island. The girl that really had my eye was the rich kid's girlfriend. She and I flirted, and even touched each other, until one night out of the blue she invited me to her house to study. We didn't even have a class together, but I accepted immediately. She lived in a more modest part of town. It was upscale but nowhere near as fancy as her boyfriend's place. Her parents both worked so we were alone. It took all of five minutes and we were in her room with the door locked. Seems she liked me a lot. She told me that – let's call him Sam (as that was his first name) – didn't share the same pleasures with her. We were less than discreet, and soon her friends and mine all figured it out. We were seen twice going under the stadium bleachers. Sam thought he was going to have his revenge.

Since I didn't make the baseball team and my grades were good, I asked for early graduation because I had to return to Winnipeg for an emergency. I had told them I was living with my aunt. Brad's mom faked that for me. In her eyes, I protected Brad from the jams he would get himself into. It was a fair trade off. I graduated early.

I had no plans to go to Winnipeg, although I did miss my brother, and my uncle

Chuck had mentioned a business opportunity in spring, there. By my low standards, I had a good life. I was holding my own. I always faced some money challenges: the lack of it to be precise. I worked more hours at the restaurant. And I did a lot more surfing, now. First thing in the mornings, my surfer girlfriend, who was older than me, found special ways to wake me. Then we would hit the waves for an hour. After we'd go to her apartment, also on the beach, but much nicer than mine for a shower. Her dad had a retail store and paid her rent. She worked there Tuesday through Saturday. We were buddies. She was cool. She loved surfing and was very good. One crazy thing we did was trying to peroxide my hair blonde. We didn't know you needed at least three treatments. The first time my hair went carrot orange. We didn't know what to do so we cut it all off. I was a skinhead for about a week. I had planned my trip to Winnipeg for late April, about two and half months away. So I was going to head to Hawaii for some big waves.

I AM GOING TO DRIVE A FERRARI

Remember I mentioned how Sam was going to get his revenge? Well, that was a half-truth. It didn't work out well for either of us. He had figured out that his girl and I were sharing something he wasn't. I'm sure plenty of people were happy to share what they knew. He knew where I worked and made a reservation for a Saturday night. His girl did not know I worked there. They walked in at 7:00 pm and I was at the meal staging station. I saw them, but they didn't see me. They were seated at one of those tables that had to pull out to be seated, then pushed back in. I was going to have to serve them water and butter. This was going to be, at best, awkward. It was my station, and the other busboy was busy. I had to do it.

He said, "Errol!" with surprise as if he was shocked to see me. "You work here? You know my lady?" He was going to stick it to me and did. She was embarrassed. I could see it on her face. He was quick to point out I was not a waiter when I gave them the menus. He also asked me questions like, what would I recommend and do they let the help try the different dishes. The waitress that was serving them came back to the serving station and asked if I saw how beautiful that girl was at table six. I didn't know how to react. I was mad, but it was my job. I knew he had planned this and was laying it on me.

When the waitresses had a heavy tray, the busboys would carry it out. We had a large table in my section, a party of three couples that were in for the lobster. I was asked to carry the tray with the waitress trailing behind with the tray stand. I would place the tray on the stand, and she'd serve, after which I'd remove the stand and tray. I had the tray with the six lobster dinners aboard, and I had to walk right past Sam's table. He casually stuck out his leg and tripped me. I fell and the dinners crashed to the ground. He was laughing. The waitress was in shock but helped me up. The owner was right on me with no words of kindness. He informed me that those dinners would come out of my pay. The toughest part was he said all this right in front of Sam's table. He also ordered me to go to the patrons' table and apologize for the delay in their dinner and inform them that I would be covering the cost of the meal. This just delighted Sam. These lobsters were twenty-five bucks a meal. Six of them equaled, more than a week's pay. As the other busboy came to help, I went to apologize to the party with the delayed meal.

I approached the table and started my apology, but one of the gentlemen sitting facing Sam's table stopped me. They had overheard the owner's reprimand, as did half the restaurant. He said he had seen the whole thing and would tell the owner, not to worry. He would straighten out the whole mess. This was music to my ears. When the owner came to their table with a complimentary bottle of wine, the customer must have done just that. Later, the boss did come to tell me I was off the hook. The other busboy took Sam's table. Later, I was bringing back a tray of dirty dishes and again passing Sam's table. They were on their desert. I will be damned if he didn't try the same trick, again. This time, I was ready and stopped just in front of his outstretched leg, looking down at it. He just laughed.

75

Sadly, for him, this sent me over the top, and I saw red. He'd pushed me to my place of reckless abandon. I returned to their table with a water pitcher, and asked if they wanted coffee. She declined. He accepted. I returned with a full pot of freshly brewed, piping hot coffee. I positioned myself at the table so he could not exit. Then, with my left hand, I, "oops," missed his cup and poured it directly into his lap. He jumped and screamed trying to stop me, grabbed my left arm. So, with my right arm, I hit him square in the mouth. Sam wore braces. I hit him like a mule. My index knuckle literally stapled his mouth to the braces, which came through his lip. She was crying. The owner rushed over me with his arm raised to strike me. I turned and warned him off in no uncertain terms. Then said, "I guess this means I'm fired." He nodded his head. Sam was taking a trip to the hospital. I wrapped my bleeding hand and walked out, leaving behind my jacket.

Was I wrong? Absolutely! Yes, I handled things badly, so I'll make no excuses.

I lived about two miles up the peninsula but just wanted some fresh air. I was standing at the side of the building when the man who had straightened out the lobster ordeal approached me. You need a job, he asked? Before I could muster an answer, he added, I own Ruben E Lees on the coast highway, know it? Well, it was a landmark, you couldn't miss it. He continued, you'll make better tips with me. He gave me his card and told me to see him tomorrow afternoon.

Wow! As I walked home I was thinking, if I'd known this was going to happen, I could have hammered Sam when he came in and been done with it. Just kidding. Things always happen for a reason. There have been many times I have not been proud of my actions, but most of those times I learned from them.

The interview went well, and he suggested I work in the car park instead of as a busboy since I would earn much better tips. He was right. This was a busier restaurant, with a nightclub on the second floor, and an upscale clientele. I worked with three Mexican boys that had been there a long time. They were good guys and showed me the ropes. I never told anyone I was fifteen and didn't have a license. I didn't understand that I was an insurance liability, nor would I have cared; the cash was rolling in. We had what was called an up system. Each of us had a set of keys to cars we parked. If you were busy parking and your client came out the other guys would cover for you and give you the tip. We all got along very well. Before our shift, we would meet in the kitchen for a meal provided us. They were funny guys, and I felt comfortable with them. We usually got a weekday off and worked the weekends, when traffic was busiest. It was Friday night, Saturday, and Sunday brunch that filled our pockets.

Okay, so, the Ferrari story. The lot was just filling up for Sunday brunch when down the coast highway came to a brand new 1965 red 330 Ferrari. We all had heard it before we saw it. Then it came into sight and geared down to turn into the parking lot. We all stopped in our tracks, gawking at this thing of beauty. At the same time, we all realized whose turn it was to park this car. You guessed it, mine!! Oh, man, are you kidding me? Am I going to park a Ferrari? As the car slowly moved toward us, my anticipation was raising. I didn't want to show my excitement, as I opened his door. The lot was full, so the next question was where exactly do you park a Ferrari? I welcomed him to Ruben E Lees. "Have a nice lunch, sir," I say, as nicely as I can, while he walked into the restaurant. I positioned myself in the driver's seat. The boys are looking at me as I rev the engine, with a smile. Sounded good. So, I did it again. Okay, so, where to park it. Close to the door or far away? Maybe in two parking spots? So many decisions: I had to drive that car around the parking lot seventy-six times before finding the right spot, in front of the door.

What kind of a tip should I expect? This is a Ferrari, so ten, no twenty bucks, for sure. When the gentleman returned, I had his keys ready, excited about my forthcoming, new fortune. He looked down and pointed out I had a hole in my white jeans. I knew there was a hole and I didn't need it pointed out. They were clean, just old.

He reached into his pocket and pulled out a wad of bills big enough to choke a horse. Oh, man, this guy was going to buy me a new pair of jeans! Instead, he peeled off a one dollar bill and handed it to me.

This was my tip, and I should have been grateful. I did show my disappointment, though, like a kid that took a lick of his ice cream cone just before it dropped off the cone, onto the ground. Picking up on my poor attitude, he pulled the bill back. He pulled out a gold cross pen and wrote: "Think and Grow Rich," N. Hill, on the bill, before returning it to me. He said that I needed an attitude adjustment. As he drove off, I waved good-bye with my middle finger, wishing I had taken his car on the coast highway to, oh, San Diego, some eighty miles away.

MR. HILL

I guess a week went by and I was at the shopping center in front of a bookstore when I pulled out that bill. I hadn't intended to save it, I just did. There it was, his note staring me in the face. I went inside and bought the book for .99 cents.

I was not much of a reader, but I couldn't put the book down. I would fall asleep reading it. I read all night Saturday after work. I called in sick Sunday and Monday, just reading this book. Tuesday, I went out and got a legal pad of paper to write out my life goals, as instructed. I bought into every word I read. Wednesday, I emerged from my little piece of crap shack and was no longer poor. I had goals and direction. I would follow the thirteen principles of success in the book and reprogram my life for riches. I moved to Hawaii, where some of my older surfer friends now lived. It was big wave season.

My Uncle Chuck had married Judy, from a prominent Winnipeg family. The brothers owned a massive company. Her youngest brother was having his Bar Mitzvah. This new family Chuck married into was tight. They were a real family. I was invited to attend by Judy. They wanted to fly me to LA and meet up with a group of entertainers that were hired to perform at the event. One was a family member. Judy's dad nicknamed Blackie, from his days delivering coal, was flying the whole group up for the Bar Mitzvah. My dad and brother were also invited. Dad picked me up at the airport and his couch was my bed. It was cold, real cold in Winnipeg. The temperature hit forty below zero.

It was a sumptuous affair. Judy was a charming lady. They seemed very happy. I met all the members of the family. They would have these Sunday brunches usually at Blackie's house. All the family attended. This was a big family: four brothers, many children. They were warm and loving. You could see they cared deeply for each other. It was nice to be in their presence. They made you feel comfortable. Chuck called Blackie dad. Hersh and I called him Uncle C as we did the other brothers, too. This family was elite.

Napoleon and his book were going to work here. I was going back to Hawaii and returning in the spring. On the island of Oahu, I lived on the North Shore, on a communal farm with six guys and eight girls. On the weekends, I hitchhiked into the city and played guitar and sang at a bar in Waikiki. I made about 300 bucks a weekend and stayed with some Pan Am stewardesses. Then I went back to the North Shore and surfed.

I had a plan for spring in Winnipeg. I was in Santa Monica visiting Aunty Betty, when she shared the news. My dad had given my brother up to Jewish Child and Welfare Serves. "Why?" I asked. We called my Aunt Thelma in Winnipeg, and she shared the story. There were plenty of families that would have and wanted to take him in. Dad wasn't getting any more sympathy and Hersh just became a burden. His ego prevented Hersh going to a family member and dad had the power to do whatever he wanted. He hung up on me when I tried phoning him. I felt so helpless and in such pain thinking of my brother in some stranger's home. He was such a good kid; he didn't deserve this.

MY FIRST TWO BUSINESS VENTURES

It was early spring of 1965, a month before my birthday. I didn't tell my dad that I was coming back to Winnipeg. My aunt Thelma picked me up at the airport, and I stayed on her couch. The first order of business was to see my brother. He was in a group home with five other boys. I was too young and broke to do anything about this situation.

I answered an ad in the newspaper to work at Palm Springs European Health Spa on Main Street. It was a ten-minute walk from Thelma's. The manager, Paul, hired me after two interviews. This was a hard sales environment. They hammered guests until they joined. Paul trained me. There was a German sales lady and a man from Vancouver. I started out working on the lady's day floor. The spa was open seven days a week. Monday, Wednesday, and Friday were the men's days. Tuesday, Thursday, and Saturday were the ladies' days. Sunday was split, morning for men, afternoon for ladies. It was a class spa in the basement of a small strip mall. The entrance led down a nice staircase to the reception and member sign in area. The gym floor was right from that area with a walkway to the lockers. They were a fully equipped wet spa with steam sauna, pool, hot tub and cold plunge. There were a large shower area and a dressing area with mirrors and toiletries laid out. There was a quiet room with comfortable recliners that they called yoga chairs.

I took to this business right away, seeing that these people were making money. I worked out all the time and was very fit, so I knew most of the exercises and learned the balance very easily. Paul, knowing I was Jewish, first put me on the ladies' floor, where most of the patrons were also Jewish. I got along with them very well.

I was a quick study and asked about sales. Paul gave me the sales manual and instructed me to learn it. I was taught how to close the spa, as we were open 9 am to 10 pm weekdays, and 9 am to 6 pm Saturday, then 10 am to 5 pm Sunday. Ken, the manager, taught me the closing procedure, which consisted of wiping down the exercise machines, putting the dumbbells on the rack then vacuuming the rich, red shag carpet. The exercise floor closed a half hour before the full spa. I started clean up there, then at closing did the locker area. The last to be cleaned was the spa area, to give the clients a chance to finish up in the shower area.

I was given the keys to the club more out of convenience to Ken. If there were no sales presentations in the three offices in the front, just off the exercise floor, he and the other sales staff would leave early. I would be left to lock up. Sure, it was more for them than for me, but I took advantage of the opportunity. This was much more comfortable than my aunt's couch. I started studying the manual and sleeping in the yoga room. I used the pool and the spa areas, too. It was my first million-dollar home. The other bonus was the other instructors, both girls, stayed for after work activities. I did get caught, once. You know when you feel you are being watched and then discover that you are? Paul came back. I guess he saw the lights on and thought the last person out had forgotten to turn them out. The exercise floor had a tall glass window at the end, looking over the pool and hot tub areas. I was in the hot tub with a staff member, performing a specific exercise. I glanced over my shoulder, and there was Paul, arms crossed. He didn't see me glance up, though, and, considering I was caught, and most likely getting fired, I just carried on. I was waiting for him to come to the spa area. When I looked again, though, he was gone.

The next day he walked past me like nothing had ever happened. I never shared his visit with my friend. Indeed, it was never discussed, until years later, after some heavy drinking – in Manhattan, New York, of all places. That's another story.

Meanwhile, with life going on as normal, Paul tested me on the manual and found I knew every page. So, he gave me my shot at sales. First, I would take prospects on a tour of facilities for the closers. And I did all the selling, there. I would ask questions about what they wanted to accomplish, why they'd let themselves get out of shape, would they dedicate a few hours a week to changing their life. Were they willing to make a $30 a month investment in themselves, for a better lifestyle? All very soft sell: but by the time I turned them over, they were ready to buy. The sales staff all wanted me to tour their guests, as it was easy money. The hell with that, I thought and went back to Paul asking for a commission. He said the person who signs the contract gets the commission. Ken and the other two sales people initially balked. I watched, though, learned how to fill out the contacts, and started closing the deals on the tour. My name on the contact got me the commissions. As you can imagine, this did not go over well with the sales staff who were soon at my throat. Paul had intervened before it got physical (they, of course, had no idea that physical conflict was my strong suit).

Paul imposed rules. The company leads went to the manager and sales staff. I could sign up referral business. These were the people I invited to the spa, using guest passes, with my name on them. Also, I gave guest passes to the current clients. The sales staff knew how to close, no question, but they were a bit on the lazy side when it came to generating business. They were more the give me fish type from the advertising. The spa had a large advertising budget, and there was always some promotion inducing people to buy now. When a member brought a guest, they would get hammered to buy in the closing office, while the members finished and dressed. This tactic resulted in members not inviting guests out of embarrassment. I could see this method was flawed. As an instructor on the floor, I got the direct feedback from the members. It pissed them off.

Finally, I saw my big chance to find a better way to sign up people, without pissing off the sales staff, and getting the commission. I went to work on this aggressively. The members liked me, so I made them allies. I told them if they brought guests and I signed them up I would get a commission. I also told them if I didn't sign the contract, I wouldn't receive the commission. I told them I would personally take care of their guests and made appointments with them to do so.

This was an unorthodox approach, but I was young and competing with more experienced people on the sales team. The clients went out of their way to help me. Even to the point, in many cases, where they had pre-sold their own guests, telling me how to handle them. I just needed to make sure they enjoyed themselves and could see the program's benefits. I would take them through the process, personally designing their program. I was getting very busy with all this, so I trained a couple of girls to do things my way. They enjoyed my process, and the complaints almost completely died off. I had built an internal machine. In a few months, I was out-producing the entire sales staff combined. My weekly commissions were larger than my monthly paychecks. I acknowledged birthdays with announcements on the loudspeaker system. Everyone would stop to sing happy birthday and give the ladies flowers: anything to make them feel special. We created a fun atmosphere. If a client did not attend, we called them and encouraged them to come back. Other members on the floor would give testimonials to the guests about how great it was, and worth the money, and how they should join. I taught the staff how to fill out the contacts, pre-signed by me. I built a small business system inside a business. This all paid off not only financially but as a business education. The traffic counts in the spa were way up and the guest traffic equally strong. The sales staff continued to close the newspaper ad traffic. It always blew me away as then they would put them out on the floor for me. I converted them to my program. The first thing I did was to take the guest pass with the sales staff's name, away and give them mine.

There were some funny incidents during this time, as well. One day, when I was working the one to ten shift, one of my old, Jewish ladies came in with a guest. These ladies always pre-sold. When they brought someone; they were coming to join. Our spa was in the basement, and we had a juice bar upstairs at the entrance. There was a beautiful staircase leading down. Ken was at the guest registration desk as this lady came down with her guest. I was told later that as he greeted them, she introduced the guest as a friend that would be joining and starting her program, today. He happily had her register on the guest sheet, then invited them in to do the paperwork. She said, "Where is Arie?" "Oh! He starts at 1:00 pm," Ken informed her. "Okay, then," she said, "We'll wait for Arie!" "Well, I can have everything done by the time he gets in," Ken continued. "Nope, I want Arie to get the commission. If he doesn't sign the contract, he doesn't get it." Ken made a few more attempts, but she wouldn't budge from her position. When I arrived, they were sitting, waiting. They both got up and greeted me with a big hug and asked if I wanted to do the contract, now. This was all in front of Ken. My ego got the best of me, and I just said we'd do it on the floor and suggested they should change, saying we'd have some fun. I smiled at Ken and grabbed my clipboard, then took contact from his hand. I thanked him for waiting for me, tongue in cheek, and walked off. Later Ken said it was his sale as he'd signed them in the guest book. Paul overruled him.

I wasn't done, yet, though. I made up boxes for guest passes at the local retailer and upstairs at the restaurant. The owner owned the whole complex. He was a Jewish man and very helpful. He had a free membership but never used it. I got him downstairs and set up a program for him. In turn, he introduced me to his clients, and we signed up many of them. I became the number one salesperson. Then I found out Ken was getting a small override on all my sales. I felt that was unfair. He was not helpful in any way, and I wanted that money. I complained to Paul but lost that battle.

I would later learn to pick my battles, but now I was young and had an immature business mind. I later made Ken a very good friend. He would be in business with me, again, twice in later life. Both times we did very well.

The other business was the second reason I came to Winnipeg. The first you'll recall was for my brother. My uncle Chuck rented trucks from a Jewish guy from time to time. I was going to need three trucks for this business. I had raised the capital from the spa commissions. I started to work the 1-9 shift and took Wednesday and the weekends off to conduct this other business.

This is a laugh; I was shoveling shit! Each spring in Winnipeg there was a great need for manure for the lawns and flowerbeds. The nurseries would sell it in five-pound bags for just under two dollars a pound. Uncle Chuck told me of a friend of his that delivered it door to door and made a fortune. The friend didn't do it anymore, but he'd raised enough seed money to start another business. I was going to try to do the same.

I had my first, rough business plan. It was a kind of "what I needed" list. I contacted the supplier and went to see them. I had two older Jewish boys working with me. They both drove, and one had access to a car. He drove me if I paid gas money. I shared a bit of the idea with them. I suggested if they wanted to put up some money they could be partners. They both declined but agreed to work for me. Next, I needed the trucks. I used my uncle's name to get them. I did all the bookings on the phone and sent my drivers to pick them up. I needed labor, so I hired three

Native Americans off the street with the promise of a case of beer a day, which was a 24 pack.

I used a vacant field close to Main Street as a staging area. I bought a bag of manure from one of the nurseries. The plan was to sell by the basket, rather than by the bag. I measured my baskets and bags against the five-pound bag I had bought, to make sure I gave value. On the first load, I shoveled it into baskets to see how many I could make. This gave me my cost per basket. It was all rough but close enough to get what I would later understand to be the cost of the goods plus a profit margin.

I went out to the farm with the driver. The trucks were five-ton and gated. We stapled cut cardboard boxes to the wood, enabling them to carry the manure. They had a scale under their hopper. They weighed the trucks and then loaded them and weighed them again. The loads were costing me between twenty and thirty dollars each. We needed a canvas to cover the load. I hadn't thought of that but uncovered there was nothing to stop the manure from blowing all over the street. The farmers showed me what to do. I gave them a one-hundred-dollar deposit, and they kept a logbook of what was owed.

I got three more canvases from my uncle's farm to place the loads in the field, which, by the way, I had no permission to use. The sales team consisted of me and another boy who I was close to. Later, he became my roommate, for a year. The others got two more friends as drivers. Off they went to get more manure and off we went to canvas an area, door to door. We each had a fulfillment book to keep track of the orders and collections. Many of the people would pay in advance, so we had the cash flow to pay for things along the way.

We ran into opportunities as this business was popular and most people liked the delivery right to their home, rather than having to lug the manure bags around. We dumped the manure right in the customer's flowerbeds. Some wanted a full truckload dumped on their front lawn and then we would charge a fee for spreading.

One man wanted us to lay sod. I went to the nursery and bought it with directions from the staff and called two landscape companies. I had them meet me on the site for a quote. Later I subcontracted to one of the companies – a cool polish guy and his son. I found out they were doing the same type of advertising as the spa. They would place their ads, give quotes and get jobs. Neither of them was sales oriented and nor closers. I went to a new development, knocked on the doors and got the jobs. They would come up behind me and complete the contacts. They also bought the manure from me as I was much cheaper than their suppliers.

I was working right out of "Think and Grow Rich," were Hill said the most important thing is just to get started and find the things you need along the way. I was changing things daily.

During this time, I was still working at the spa. It was funny, the staff knew what I was doing and made me shower before coming on the floor. I had a spot in the alley for my dirty cloth and shoes. I would come down the back stairs in a towel to the showers. On lady's days, I went to my aunt's and changed there. The staff, especially Ken, got the biggest laugh. He called me shit boy. If he knew how much money I was making, he would have shit! On my off days, and the weekends, I did most of the selling and paid our bills. I was paying the truck company in cash, and that was one of my slip-ups, as Uncle Chuck eventually caught me. I didn't realize that even if I paid them, they would send a monthly statement to Chuck's office. One day after I had finished with my venture he called me up to his office. I guessed that his bookkeeper finally showed him the bills. She asked why he was paying in cash. He had the invoices and the contact on his desk where I could see it. He asked me if there was anything I wanted to tell him. I was busted and, I must say, a little scared. I knew I had done wrong. Chuck also had a reputation for being pretty tough.

I told him the whole story, start to finish. He asked why I didn't come to him with the idea? He would have helped me, he added. The truth was, I didn't want to risk his saying no. He scolded me, and deservedly so, but I could see that he also was proud of me. I told him my plans for returning to Hawaii, after the summer. He wanted me to go to college with Judy's (his wife) brother, Jackie. This opened a can of worms too soon for me to react. I never told Jackie, or his cousins, who I thought I was close with, about the manure business.

Later, I did tell Chuck that I netted $28,000. I gave him a check for the money he had fronted me and for a dental bill he had paid, which my dad could not. I was so proud to give him that check. It was over a dinner with him and Judy. She was a wonderful organizer. She loved family and had a great family to love.

I ran into a few issues along the way. The business just lasted two months of spring. I learned to strike while the iron was hot. By summer sales dropped off.

I spent my birthday on the lot, with my crew of now five Indians Native Americans and three Jewish drivers and my one sales guy, drinking beer. We all got drunk, and

I had them all over to the spa after closing. I did have the key!!!!! We all had a ball. I would close the business first week in June. I carried my bankbook everywhere with such pride. I did my aunt's house for free and took my brother and the other boys at the group home out for ice cream. I didn't spend much. I had gotten along with so little for so long. I didn't know how to spend. To this day, I find it easier to buy things for others than myself. I also never shared my experience with my dad. Chuck would tell him what a great kid I was and that infuriated him. I think Chuck knew that and did it out of spite. It went back to something from when they were kids. Chuck later told me, and I left it there. That summer, my brother often came to the farm with me. His situation still pained me. I never understood why my father did it. Nor did I forgive him for what he had done to this precious young soul.

Errol has been monumental in helping build my company and keeping me on track to success. As a stay at home mom, I started my business as a hobby to make extra money for my family. My business has grown from a hobby into a very successful business in less than a year. Errol has helped me realize my most valuable asset is time and he has taught me how to "buy back my time." This has allowed me to focus my time on creativity which is why my business is thriving and why I love going to work every day. Errol truly has one of the biggest hearts I know and goes out of his way to make sure I succeed. I am excited and blessed to continue to have Errol mentor me and look forward to another year together.

Thank you, Errol!
Kristina Tamas
CEO Infinity Collection
Infinity-Collection.com

MY ROAD TO REAL ESTATE

As the leaves turned colors and the temperature dropped, I was missing surfing and my friends. I realized that Winnipeg was not my home. These people were not my real family. They were friendly enough, in fact, super people, but I felt like, and was, an outsider.

Jackie wanted to go to the University of Miami. We planned to go together. Chuck and Judy would pay my way. Jackie and I got close that year. His grades were not high enough for entry, though. I was relieved when he wasn't accepted. I had agreed under a little pressure from Chuck, who I didn't want to disappoint. Also, I did want to fit into this new family.

Jackie applied then to a California junior college in Ventura and was accepted. I applied to San Diego State and was also accepted. We had one big incident with my dad, who was still driving a cab for Chuck. My dad told him that I'd said Chuck was trying to buy me to hang out with his family by paying for my college. Chuck blew his stack at me. I confronted my dad, who justified his lies because he was Chuck's brother and should be the one benefiting from his money. It shouldn't have been me. I never understood how a father could not care about his kids and even do things to hurt them, as mine did with my brother. I convinced Chuck of the truth. Although he never apologized, that was not his style; he knew my dad was capable of such things. Chuck knew it was not in my character to say what my father had alleged.

After "Think and Grow Rich," my next mentor book was "The Very, Very Rich and How They Got That Way." I read it like a study book, as I had Hill's. It said the richest people in the world, other than those inheriting family wealth, got so through real estate.

There was an insurance man who came to the high school in those days to show us the value of insurance. I had a personal interview with him where he tried to close me on an annuity policy. He showed me how for just 20 dollars a month I could be worth a million dollars at retirement age, sixty-five. My question to him was, how do I even know if your company will be around and will have the million to give me? This was a legitimate objection from a fifteen-year-old with no business experience. He told me the insurance company invests in real estate holdings, like office buildings, malls, etc. They would have plenty of money from the growth of all these assets. That convinced me. I went to Antelope Valley and bought a five-acre lot for $4995 with $500 down and a $20 monthly mortgage. I was a property owner. Years later I would listen to Arnold Schwarzenegger's book on CD; it turned out that he and his partner, Franco Columbu, bought their first property in the same area. There was an airport planned that would absorb the excess traffic from Los Angeles International Airport (LAX). The roads were even built for it, but it was scrapped. I had a cousin that made a fortune developing the area during the excitement phase.

I returned to California and planted myself in San Diego's Mission Beach area, living with a surfer friend Doug from Lido Beach, New York. Doug was good looking and a talented surfer. He was the best of the crew. His parents subsidized him, so we had the nicest digs. It was the place everyone gathered. I had a bank role and could afford my share of the rent. I also got a job stocking shelves and bagging groceries at a large chain grocery store. That kept my bank account growing. I made enough to pay my way and still bank a few dollars. I didn't know then how to make my money work for me, so I settled for collecting my bank interest. We were still spinning records in those days, and Doug had the collection. He was a music buff. Doug had all the latest hits, but Smoky Robinson was his favorite. He would set up the music, and I would cook. His parents visited us the first Thanksgiving. They were cool people. He had a sister and a knockout girlfriend. It was no surprise that she was a model. We all got on great. His mom was a real protective type. We came home from surfing one day to discover she had stocked our fridge and cupboards with food. We had a big feast, inviting the neighbors and the other New York boys. We borrowed tables and chairs, making a big table in the living room. We had an upper, two bedrooms one bath, in a row of bungalows right by the beach. It was roomy, and our bedrooms had a view of the waves. Doug had a decked-out VW van. Inside it had a bed and storage for the surfboards. It was a real surf van, and we had some great trips.

He was at SD State, too. After classes had started, I went to the athletic department with my credentials and asked for a scholarship. I was in the best shape of my life. They called my coaches but were concerned I hadn't played during my senior season. I didn't want to revisit why that was, so I just explained that my dad had moved, so I had to transfer schools, making me ineligible for the last season. They also didn't like that I surfed and they had rules about that. Plus, my reputation as a troublemaker and fighter followed me. Eventually, they did offer a conditional scholarship. I had no one to help me analyze it and just declined. I don't know if that was a mistake or not, even to this day. The next move I made, was a defining point in my life. It was a tough decision, though. I loved sports and missed the team camaraderie. Feeling a bit dejected about all this, I booked a trip to Hawaii. It was big wave season so, since I didn't think I could afford college without that scholarship, I dropped out. I paid Doug three months' rent in advance, and he dropped me at the airport. I had many friends in Hawaii and was offered a bed in Haleiwa on the North Shore with Steve, one of the best surfers I knew. You did have to watch Steve; he was a bit of a scammer and would be happy to spend your money if you let him. His mom was a gem. She lived on a boat in town, close to Waikiki. I spent many a night sleeping on that boat. Doug's friend, the best surfer of the group, was a shaper who built surfboards. He wanted to shape a board for this trip. We agreed on $135, but he broke the tail of the blank. He repaired it, and it would work, but you can't charge for that kind of work. Since there was no time for him you build a new one, he gave it to me. I used it once, but it was way too light for big waves.

Two of the big wave riders were businessmen and shared a good deal in town. I went in to check it out as real estate was my new interest. The deal was solid. The owner of a large hotel project was selling off fifty marina condominiums to raise funds to complete the hotel. They were selling for $19,800 each. They were two bedrooms with a den and two bathrooms. The view looked over the boats in the marina with the top floor having an ocean view. I had paid off the land in Antelope Valley. I did not understand leverage but was about to get a lesson. The realtor was a local guy. I told him I had $20,000+ to spend. These businessmen had their own finance package; they just wanted fifty names to show the bank so their funds could be released to complete the building. The realtor told me I should take ten units, with ten per cent down on each, and they would rent them out to cover the costs with a little profit left over each month. This proposal was a complete surprise to me as my intention had been to pay cash for one unit. I did have to admit that his plan sounded better. I faked as if I understood him. These were agreements for sales, something you see very little of today. They did the agreement for ten units, and I put down ten percent on each. They agreed to rent out the units. The agreement formed a rental pool. I semi-understood, but not really. Sounded like a good deal to me.

This was a case of being in the right place at the right time. They sold off the fifty units that week. I was just lucky to get in the way of this deal, as it was prime property. The first payment was due in ninety days. I had enough money for about two payments. The units were rented out the first month, and I had a little profit each month. What a deal to run into. They just needed to show equity for the balance of the funds. They did the rentals and paid out the profits each month. When the hotel was opened, these units became part of the hotel's room rental inventory. This was an early version of executive apartments.

The realtor was doing an assembly for the owner. I just lucked out, plain and simple. He became a good friend of mine, over the years. He was a smart guy that knew his real estate and was involved in many deals. He educated me on how to leverage and parlay my money, just as he had, here. Now, I owned $198,000 in real estate for only $19,800. And, of course, he made a handsome commission on the deal.

Later, he would sell a unit for me so I could pay off the notes. This left me with nine units free and clear and a nice rental income. I would go to Winnipeg to see my brother and make more money.

During those two years, we did some flips and each time I made cash. I used my original nine units as collateral against the loans. He would sell them, making the commission twice, once selling to me and the other selling for me. He used my equity to secure the deals. I didn't mind; I was making money, too. This market was growing.

I plunged each profit back into the next deal, so I was real estate rich, but cash poor. On paper, I looked good. I needed more cash though to make more deals. I also missed my brother, so was thinking about heading back to Winnipeg.

There was a downside to this realtor partner. He had three weaknesses: ladies, gambling, and booze. He drove a Jaguar

2x2 and had a string of beautiful women. He knew all the local celebrities. He was connected. Yet, most of the local business people wouldn't back him, as they knew he was a drunk. As a young, want-to-be real estate investor, I didn't care about any of that. So, knowing my equity, he used me to flip these deals. The good thing was that he always needed the money, so he would sell the deals as fast as we bought them. In the process, I was getting an education on real estate deals. There was no question; this guy was a super salesman. If he could have gotten control of his vices, he would have owned half of Oahu. He also kept asking me for loans, but as I said I didn't have any cash lying around to lend him. That was a blessing in disguise, as it turned out. He owed everyone money.

During this time, I returned to California and wrapped up with Doug, at the apartment. One of the New Yorkers took my place. It was a good ending and years later I would attend Doug's wedding in New York. He would visit me in Hawaii, but the big waves were not his cup of tea.

BACK IN WINNIPEG

I drove up to Winnipeg with Jackie in his new GTO. I had visited him a few times in Ventura. There were some good winter surf breaks in his area He had been down to San Diego, as well. He had a great apartment and seemed to be enjoying school. We spoke often. Was he my cousin or uncle? His sister, Judy, Chuck's wife, was my aunt. I'm not sure what that made Jackie. I called his whole family uncle and cousin. I wanted to fit in and be a part of it. We picked up another relative, in San Francisco, for the drive up. We took one of my surfboards, which we were going to pull behind his boat at Falcon Lake, where his dad and each of his uncles had a cottage.

I wanted to see my brother, but now I had to make an appointment through the Jewish Child and Welfare office. I was informed of this policy while standing at the door, Friday afternoon, carrying gifts for all the kids. The office didn't open until Monday. The staff was comprised of college psyche majors, getting credits for working with these underprivileged children. All I ever saw them do was drink coffee and smoke cigarettes in the kitchen. They were not going to break protocol, even after my brother saw me and ran to the door for a hug. Further, they wouldn't even let me drop off the packages.

I was headed for a shit storm with this crew. There was already a scene at the door as they pushed Hersh inside. Meanwhile, I dropped by the spa to see if I could get some work. Paul was happy to see me and booked a schedule on the ladies' floor for three days a week. He had a full staff, and I was glad to have the work. Monday, bright and early, I was at JCW office and delighted that I got to wait two hours to see the boss. I asked if he could bend the new rules and let me drop by, as I lived in the area, and had a job, so I wanted to spend as much time with Hersh as possible. Hersh was nine now. I could smell smoke on him. He said that it was the other kids, knowing how I hated smoking, but I knew it was him. I was so unexcited to find that my dad, who visited once a month, left a deck pack of smokes for the kids. I called him on it and he said he was smoking at that age and to mind my own business.

Hersh was a resourceful kid. He ran away all the time. At night, he would show up at the local coffee house in the North end. He would bum smokes and then hide them with some BS story that he was on a night pass. I liked his ingenuity, so that would land him a burger and ice cream before I walked him home.

It was bound to happen, though. One day I showed up, and Hersh stank. He had pooped his pants. He had a problem with that and bedwetting. I told one of the male staff members that I would take him upstairs to shower and change. I told that was not the procedure. When Hersh realized he had done wrong, he went to clean himself. I had heard this the week before when "Fuck the Staff" had been written on the wall. I offered to wash it off but got the same story. It was still on the wall.

That day there was three male staff in the kitchen. This protocol was BS. I took Hersh upstairs and showered him, found

116

some fresh clothes and changed him. I took a wet rag and was halfway through cleaning the wall when a big guy interrupted my work. "We told you not to interfere with our discipline," he said. You have no training, I responded. You don't need much to clean a wall. See it's easy. He then did the worst thing he could have done. He grabbed me, to throw me out. I went into the red zone, and he was down in a minute, along with the other two staff who came at me. When the police arrived, after the ambulance had taken away two of them, I was taken to the cop shop. There, dear old Aunty Thelma collected me. She was not a happy camper. Whenever she started a sentence with "Arie Abramson..." I knew she is mad. There was no hearing my side. Those boys were seriously injured. But, Aunty, I protested, there was three of them. She gave me no quarter. The next day, Hersh showed up at her house. He needed a haircut, so I was instructed to get him a cut then return him to the home.

The barber found lice in his hair and refused to cut it. He asked us to leave. When we go back to Auntie's house she started to cry. I asked her to call her doctor's office. They got us to a dermatologist. I called the home; they referred me to the JCW office. There, the head guy wanted to see me after the doctor's appointment.

We got a prescription to kill the lice. I went to the meeting with the director of JCW, and he made light of the lice. I didn't like his attitude or his staff, and I told him so. He got mad and told me to fuck off. I went red, and Aunty Thelma bailed me out again.

There was a hearing to see if we would go to trial. They read the complaints. The prosecution stated their case. I defended myself, against the judge's warning, as these were serious charges. They presented evidence from the staff. The head of JCW was in court, too. He was a lawyer. I just told the judge what had happened. He asked the other side if they wanted to pursue this. Before they answered, he again said I would need representation. He suggested that he would come down off the bench and defend me himself. He said he had been a pretty good defense lawyer before his appointment to the bench. The prosecution suggested that if he were to give me a stern reprimand that would be sufficient. He acknowledged my love of my brother, and applauded my defending him, but said my behavior was a tad extreme. I was instructed to behave myself on future visits. I agreed.

I know I did not handle things correctly. I was just frustrated with the fact that I could not rescue my brother. This was a lifetime wound that would be reopened again and again.

GET THE CASH

The spa had a full staff and though Paul gave me hours, it was not nearly enough to make the commissions I'd previously earned. I didn't want to shovel the shit, again, either. My uncle Chuck's father in law, Jackie's dad, asked if I wanted to work for him at their offices. Chuck had told him I was a fine worker. I didn't know what I was going to do. One of the other cousins, Bernie, was working for them that summer as a surveyor. This was family and full time. So, I took the job.

It was a huge property. They were the largest road construction company in Canada. I couldn't even imagine, with all the heavy equipment and buildings what, the company was worth. The facility was at least 50 if not 100, acres. In the front was a large two-story office building. The first day, I was escorted to Blackie's office. It was large and well appointed. The reception area had a workstation. His assistant, a very pleasant lady, rang to inform him his nephew had arrived. Wow! Nephew!! He came to the door and smiled. "Come in, Arie." He always had time for me. He was such a nice man. Inside, there was a beautiful large desk, full of work, a seating area with a couch, two chairs, and a table with six chairs, also stacked with files. I would later find out that he and his team did most of the costing and bidding on big contracts. Then they purchased the equipment and supplies needed to complete the contracts.

I could not believe the way he treated me. He took me over to the couch and sat me down, offering me a pop or coffee. I took water. His assistant brought him a coffee and me a bottle of water. He wanted to chat. This busy man, running this huge company, was asking me a personal question about my life. I was blown away by his kindness. He said that he was sorry about the work they found for me this summer, but it would pay well. We chatted for about an hour on simple subjects: California and surfing, Jackie's cool car, and other stuff a dad would talk to his kid about. He thanked me for coming in. Wow, thanked me! Then he rang a man who took me to the warehouse. See you Sunday, Arie. That would be for brunch.

I passed Bernie in the hall. He said, "Let's meet for lunch." He went into the field to survey, but returned for lunch, at the corporate dining room. Bernie was the son of Abe, the youngest of the brothers, and head of the company's legal counsel. Abe's offices were downtown. He was a QC and very respected in the community, I later learned. There were three boys, the older was away at MIT, Bernie was in the middle, and Murray was the youngest. I hung out with the two younger boys and Jackie throughout the summer. They were family – so I thought.

My job was interesting, to say the least. First, I got to know the warehouse crew. This was the dispatch center. Here the different crews out on jobs would call in with their needs for equipment or supplies. Many times a day the foremen or project managers would come in with their list of things needed for the job. The dispatch man was the warehouse boss. He ran the yard, the warehouse, and all the deliveries. There were millions and millions of dollars of heavy equipment parked all over the place. There were two truck drivers for the eighteen-wheeler and the larger equipment. They were on call and, when not working, gathered together play cards.

The dispatcher was my immediate boss. He knew I was somehow a relative of the owners, but never asked it, and I never spoke of it, either. This huge complex was surrounded by an eight-foot high chain link fence. My job was to paint the entire fence with a galvanized silver paint. How exciting! The first job though, was to clear all the foliage and weeds from the bottom. Then, I applied two coats of paint. This job, was to take all summer, and I would be getting another laborer next week. There was one big guy there, very well built. Later, I found out he was a bodybuilder and the son of one of the truck drivers. I was shown the tools for the weeding and given an electric cart. Shown once what to do and then I was left alone.

After all of this was arranged, I met with Paul and told him I had a summer job that paid better. I needed the money. He understood and asked if I would be there in the fall. I told him I didn't know but would stop by from time to time.

I rented a two-bedroom basement with one of my Jewish friends from the manure business. It was a bit of a dump, but we made it work. Like in Newport Beach, it became the place to hang at night. Again, all my cousins lived at home, so we became the party house. Bernie would swing by and pick me up some days. Others, I would take the 20-minute bus ride. We spent a lot of time together. Jackie also had a summer job, at the downtown office.

About a week later, I was well into the job. At first, I took a little ribbing from the warehouse guys, especially the big, young bodybuilder. He once changed my hard hat, which was mandatory headgear, from the yellow laborer to a white supervisor's one. It brought a big laugh. As a supervisor, I ordered him to work, to an even bigger laugh. For the most part, they were good guys. They saw I worked hard and respected that. The only other deal was at lunchtime. They all brought their lunch box and met at a spot in the warehouse, with a few tables and a soda machine.

They ate, then played cards until the dispatcher got up: then lunch was over. For me, the first day, I was about to dig into my egg salad sandwich when Bernie showed up. "Arie let's go to lunch," he said to some snide remarks.

We entered the building and when to the executive lunch cafeteria. It was just a little smaller than the one at Newport Harbor High. There was a huge selection. Bernie had coupons for us. We selected anything we wanted. Everyone there eating was in a business dress, the men in suits and ties, the wore women smart business dresses. We were the only ones there dressed in laborer's clothes. I was especially on the grubby side. In the morning, he made a point of telling me if his crew would be back for lunch. It was very rare he wasn't. If not, though, I ate in the warehouse. If so muscles got my lunch. Or, if he didn't want it and he would ask what it was, I would take it out in the yard.

My new work partner showed up a week later. This kid was also juiced in. He was a beauty. I don't think he'd done a day's work in his life. The first day out, we were clearing, and all he did was complain about how hard the work was. He said he didn't know it was going to be manual labor. He was in college and thought he should have been wearing a suit. He didn't like the work and complained that he didn't know how he would make it through the whole summer. I worked hard. He would be on one side of the fence, and I would go clear on the other side. I was always way ahead and then came back to finish up with him. At one point, he commented that this was obviously my calling. I was meant to be a laborer, but not him. No doubt, he earned a knuckle sandwich, but what was the point. He was no fighter. I did tell him to zip it, once. He got the message. He lasted all of one week. The next Monday, I was back on my own.

When I was three-quarter done with the clearing, the paint was ordered. In the morning, I'd have coffee with the guys in the dispatch office. It was a large open office with three people working at their own desks. The dispatcher had a walkie-talkie to all the jobs. The morning needs would blast across the system, and one by one the guys would be off to fill the orders. This was our ritual. When an order would come in, he would write it in a logbook. He used a ruler to make an x though the job when it was filled. I share this because a few times he was late. No one knew what to do. I put on his white hat and started taking the orders. I managed the logbook just like he did. One job needed a D-9 bulldozer, and I sent the driver to hook a lowboy trailer for loading and transport. I sent muscles to get the dozer, check it out and fuel it for release. They all listened to me. He came in an hour late and to his surprise, all was in order.

He just looked at me like WTF and smiled. I put his hat on him and drove off. This was an interesting day. I was turning the corner of the property, heading for the front of the building. I found out that day that Bernie's dad, Abe, and Saul, the oldest brother, worked at the downtown executive offices where Jackie was. This day, they were all there, lounging in the executive boardroom. I didn't even know they had one. Bernie and Jackie were having lunch there with the brass. They came over to say hello. Jackie was wearing a very nice suit. Bernie gave me the lunch pass and said he'd see me after work. We had party plans that evening.

I entered the cafeteria. As usual, now, all the servers knew me by name. Most of the executives would say hello. It was a nice, friendly atmosphere. Today, though, was going to be different. A Vice President came to my table and ordered me out. I was not an executive with this firm, he said. I was shocked. After swallowing my food, I asked who he was? He blurted out his title and again ordered me to leave, adding that I shouldn't return. Let the kid finish his lunch. Ben, one of the suits said. He stood fast, though. I was so embarrassed, but this was not the place for my usual reaction. Oh, though, did I want to drop this guy. I left, head down, without incident.

I was almost crying by the time I crossed the parking lot for the warehouse. I just grabbed my hard hat and went back to work. Bernie was informed about the incident as I left the lunch pass with the girls. Later, he said the guy was an owner of a medium size company they had acquired. He was pretty good at what he did, but that conduct today was uncalled for. He also explained the other kid on my crew was the guy's son. They didn't have another job for him. I told Bernie what I had wanted to do; he said he wished I had. This guy was bitter, as he thought he should have been better paid for the purchase of his company. He wasn't to be trifled with, though. He parked in the row of executive cars. So, he was somebody.

I brought my lunch the next day even though Bernie wanted me to come with him. He figured this guy was waiting for an opportunity to go again and knew where Bernie would be for lunch that day. He felt he wouldn't try it again in front of Abe's kid. I just didn't want to face that kind of embarrassment, again. So I had lunch with the warehouse staff.

A voice rang out about fifteen minutes later. Anyone seen my nephew, Blackie called. He came to the lunch area. He knew the guys and BS'ed with them a bit. "Arie, can you have lunch with me today?" he asked. What was I going to say no?

129

While we crossed the lot, he said, "I understand you have all the clearing done." He'd thought that would take a month and a half to complete. He knew how much work I had done. We entered the cafeteria and sitting at the same table was Ben, my evictor. Blackie walked right up to him and said, "Thanks for joining me. Oh, have you met my nephew, Arie? He's working for us this summer." Ben said nothing, nor did I. I thanked Blackie and never stepped in that cafeteria again.

I finished the fence in one month. They had brushes for the job, but I bought a large roller and found it did the links much more efficiently. I used the brushes for the poles. Blackie made me a contractor and paid me the equivalent of two workers, working three months. He then got me a job in Gillem, Manitoba.

GOING NORTH TO GILLEM

I was called to an interview at the Manitoba Hydro offices. It seemed that the interview was a formality. I was hired and scheduled to leave that week. Gillem was some 660 miles North of Winnipeg. This was the Nelson River Dam project. I flew in on a small twin-engine, 12-seater. I was hired to work for Manitoba Hydro as a soil inspector. I did know what soil was. Everything else I learned on the job.

Gillem was a small Indian (Native American) community. Hydro had built a large Community Center in town with a hockey rink, bowling alley, movie theater and a host of other amenities. There were houses built for the locals as well as a small development for the senior staff and their families. There was a hotel and a pub along with a few other local businesses. The largest was the Hudson Bay Company outpost, attached to the community center. And let us not forget the RCMP station, which I would get to know, well.

The camp itself was a few miles outside of the town. It consisted of several rows of trailer housing set up for 1800 men, usually two per room. We, at hydro, had our own trailer with private rooms. Toilets and showers were in the middle of each trailer. There were several other buildings, like the dining hall, a small like malt shop where you could get a burger, and an attached general store selling toiletries and over the counter medications. They had a great gym. And there was a social hall, with about 10 round tables that were used for gambling. This always cracked me up, as there was a big sign declaring "no gambling allowed" hung over the tables where they played cards and gambled.

The kitchen was staffed on contract by a Montreal firm. They provided a chef, cooks and kitchen staff. All the servers were women. I found out that they were there for a dual purpose.

The labor force was mixed, but mostly tradesmen, up for good money. The project work was a 24/7 affair. I worked two weeks of days and then two of nights. It was a twelve-hour day. All food was provided, and you were either bussed back to the dining hall, or a lunch wagon would come out. The hydro workers had our own vehicles and always ate in the dining hall.

As this was Hydro's project, all the other companies were contracted and working for us. We were equivalent to the police or building inspectors of the project work. We had a staff of over one hundred engineers, plus us kids filling spots. Then we employed the subcontractors, also for inspection. Like the survey teams, the contractors sent out their team, and ours followed. It was a massive project.

As mentioned, I was a soil inspector. The abutments that were built on each side of the several dams and power stations had a building code, stipulating density per square foot. The layers of these abutments had to be tested. Again, the contractor had a team and so did we. Our team counted. If the contractor didn't pass our tests, they had to reroll the area until the proper density was reached. This was a huge bone of contention with the foremen. A repack took time and could throw them off schedule. As you can imagine, we were unpopular with these old, veteran contractors. They considered us a pain in the ass. But we had our own foremen, and they had the power to shut down the job until things met code. Most of our foremen came from the private sector and considered themselves lucky to have a government job. They were right. There were a lot of perks with the position. It was like being a turncoat in the eyes of the contractors. Many times, they would yell at each other. Often the contractors would sarcastically remind our foremen, "Remember when you had to work for a living?" The reply would be something like, "Yeah, and got paid that shit salary you get." Then they would all go to the pub and buy each other beers. It was all quite civilized and very humorous at the same time.

The term pub might be a bit misleading. The pub in camp was the largest pub in Canada. It seated over a thousand drinkers. Hydro flew in weekend acts. The beer and wine flowed, too. If you wanted a hard drink, you brought your own bottle and poured under the table. The RCMP were around and could enforce the rules, but usually, would sit and drink with us.

There were some rules strictly enforced, like no fighting. The person that was deemed the instigator was removed from camp on the next plane out. Other infractions I learned about along the way.

There was a huge camp gym with all the latest equipment. It was only outdone by the community center gym and spa, in town. I worked out a lot and made two great friends, both body builders. Gerry and Ross were two great guys. Both were engineers in structural design, working for one of Hydro's subcontractors. Gerry was Polish and what a body. He was a big guy, six-four, and was training for Mr. Canada, the same as Ross. They were workout partners but allowed me to join in on sets with them. I, in turn, taught them martial arts. I had black belts in two disciplines. There was also a Jujitsu black belt in the camp. He taught, as well. Soon, the RCMP started training with us. They had been taught some skills, but not as much as today. Also, in those days, you had to be a certain height and weight to land a job up north. I got to know the guys well, and that came in handy for my future business ventures.

In each trailer, there was a "boil cook." These men cleaned the trailers' common area and made all the beds, changing the sheets every two days. They were the lowest on the pay scale, only working a few hours each shift. They were the best-dressed, coolest guys in camp. They were all the gamblers. They would set up and play the card games, strike, five and seven-card stud, poker, blackjack and more. My boil cook, Ted, was the coolest of them all. He educated me about a lot going on in the camp and the town.

Both Ross and Gerry took vacations to travel to Montreal and compete in the Mr. Canada contest. The promoters of the event were Ben and Joe Weider. Later in life, I interviewed them both for a magazine I owned. I had seen muscular guys at the beach before, but nobody like these two. They were ripped. They had supplements and protein bars shipped in from Weider's company in Montreal. They had a very specific diet. Gerry would order 12 scrambled eggs and sometimes go back for another dozen. On their camp regime, you could eat as much as you wanted.

They returned to a big celebration, as Gerry won Mr. Canada and Ross won Best Chest. I would later rent a beautiful apartment with Ross for one summer in Winnipeg.

My paychecks from this job were as huge, as Uncle Blackie suggested they would. There were more opportunities, and I was determined to find them. Ted was a ladies' man, but there weren't a lot of ladies in camp. There were only those in the kitchen and the malt shop. Then, there was the town with the local girls, plus some of the wives of husbands working long hours. I learned from Ted that all the ladies in the camp were working girls. He had to explain what that meant. I couldn't get the concept; all my lady friends were happy to give it up for free. Well, it was a supply and demand situation. The lady that checked us in at our meals and her husband, a head cook, ran the girls. I was friends with them, the madam and camp pimp. They were making a fortune. He had a bar in his room and was the only one in the camp that had women in his room – not actually allowed.

In town, they had two vans beside the pub. The seats were removed with curtains dividing the front and back doors and a mattress in each section. He also had a huge selection of porn magazines for sale. Not that you couldn't order your own, as many did, but he had them in camp for sale. He even brought up women from Winnipeg for the weekends. He was a funny, little, high-energy guy. The wife and a few of the girls attended my martial arts classes, so I fulfilled my needs in trade.

Ted introduced me to his best clients: the fifty-ton truck drivers. They were among the highest paid in camp and did most of the gambling at Ted's table. Oh, yeah, it was that organized. Many of the boil cooks went from camp to camp running the games.

I got to know a few of the drivers, and they shared what their checks looked like. They made mine pale in comparison. They started at eighteen bucks an hour for the first forty hours and thirty-six for the next twenty. Remember this was twelve hours a day, seven days a week. So their last twenty-four hours were at triple time. They were grossing 12-14k a month. And, this, remember was 1966. That was monster money.

Since I was up there anyway, putting in the same time, but for less pay, I felt I had to get some of that action.

WHAT OPPORTUNITIES COULD I FIND?

Truck driving was the first thing I went after. I didn't know how to handle those big rigs, though. They were running fifty-ton Euclid's and fifty-ton Kenworths. I talked to as many drivers as I could, and the consensus was the Kenworth was the better drive. My disadvantage was I didn't know how to drive one and I'd just gotten my license. To my mind, that was a minor problem. I had a plan. These guys loved beer and women. Since I worked for Hydro, I was considered a part of the female anatomy that was referred to if you were weak on the job. Ok, I didn't want to say "pussy," but that's what they thought of me. One of the heavy machine operators was a cool guy. He was a hippy type; just up there for the bankroll. He had been to California and even tried surfing. He was raised on a farm outside of Winnipeg and learned how to operate all the equipment. He had worked for the season last year and bought a house. He intended to do the same this year. He earned about what the drivers did but liked his job better. There was too much bouncing around in those cabs. It was rough on the kidneys, he said.

My attitude was considerably different. I would donate a kidney for the kind of money those truckers made. I got close to the drivers with two pitchers of beer. They could afford their own, of course, but liked mine better.

When I worked the day shift, after dark, I flagged down one of the drivers. He would give me some lessons and then I would drive half a shift for him. After two weeks of this, I was ready. They set me up with the foreman, a cool grandfatherly type. He took me out in both trucks and asked me where I learned to handle these rigs. I said, "On the farm."

He approved me and sent me down to Winnipeg to join the union and get my safety certificate. It was just a formality; they were short three drivers at the time. I guess I didn't understand human nature, with all that money there for the taking.

Another opportunity arose when the television and radio cables came in from

Thompson, a much more established mining town. The Hudson Bay Company was starting to sell TVs and stereo equipment, records and more. I went down to the Bay, and the prices were out of this world.

I was going to be going down to Winnipeg so my Uncle Chuck's friend, who supplied the Bay, agreed to see me. I told him I felt I could make a lot of sales from within camp if he would make me competitive with the Bay. He could if he wanted. I called Uncle Chuck and invited him to Oscars for a corn beef sandwich. I told him what I was doing with the truck driving. He liked
the idea but gave me a twenty-minute unfavorable dissertation on unions. He asked if I left Hydro on good terms since Blackie had gotten me the job. I had, in fact, told them what I was doing. It was their camp, and if I angered them, they could kick me out. They were not mad at all. We were overstaffed with students, so it was just fine. The foreman said it was a good move.

Chuck did more than call his friend. He took me down to see him. The business guys struck a deal in front of me. I ordered ten units that day, to be shipped up by train. This normally took a week. I would have to do something with the stock when it got there. He gave me terms net thirty. This really worked, as I was going to get cash from the buyers. On the way home, Chuck schooled me on the importance of promptly paying, as credit is your word. I didn't tell Chuck about the Hawaii property. I owed so much money I feared he'd be angry with me.

I flew back up north two days later, with my driving certificate and my union card. I was a teamster just, like my Dad. I never shared that with him, though. I had two issues to resolve: getting my shipment to camp and where to put it. I wasn't in a single room anymore, but I knew all the hydro guys that were. I spoke to Ted first. I ended up giving him a fifty percent discount from the Bay price if he let me store the stuff in his room. He picked a TV and large stereo console. This was my first sale. Next, I visited the pimp. He was a wheeler-dealer and made me an offer. He would sell ten TVs and get his free. Next day he ordered ten: one for his wife's room and nine more for the girl's rooms. They all had plenty of dough. I sold five stereo units to his girls, too. Ted helped me get the other boil cooks to buy TVs. They had a lot of time on their hands and TV or music would help them pass the day.

They all knew the Bay prices and would get me the serial number of the unit they wanted. I gave them a thirty percent discount. The pimp had a van and, for a price, he arranged delivery and set up. This became crazy throughout camp. Everyone wanted something for their rooms. I sold the head chef a unit package. I didn't want to sell in town; I thought the Bay would find out. I went into the store and saw that they were turning their inventory, too. I talked to the salesman on the floor, an older guy. He showed me what were the most popular items.

I used his information to redesign my packages. My friends at Hydro didn't have the money to buy and were leaving at the end of summer, so had no use for the stuff. Most of the buyers had the funds to ship their purchases home or just abandon them when they left. Hydro bought several TV units from the Bay for the common areas in camp. When it hit, and the cable opened, you could walk down any trainer hallway and hear music or TV shows. I never got into the record sales. This would be my first of many missed opportunities.

This leads to my next cash cow. Ted gave me the idea. The weekends were the party time in camp. These men would consume liquor by the barrel full. The boil cooks would always bring a bottle or two to their respective tables for their suckers to drink. Most of them never touched the stuff. They were gamblers with a specific purpose. In Manitoba, we had a blue law; Sunday was a dry day. These men in a bush camp wanted to drink. They would empty out their lockers but always wanted more. Personally, I thought it was a stupid law, and some years later it was repealed.

What I also learned was the guys, by late afternoon Sunday were drunk and indifferent to what they drank. I started with six bottles of Five Star Whisky. It was the cheapest rotgut there was for sale. Ted said the guys would pay fifty dollars a bottle when they ran out. He was right. You must remember; there were five to thirty thousand dollars on each table controlled by the gamblers (the boil cooks). I walked in Sunday afternoon with my six bottles. Ted yelled, "Errol, do you have a bottle?" "I brought six," I answered. He held up fifty bucks, and I gave him one. He opened it and passed it around. There were ten guys at his table, and the bottle went once around it. The guys then would throw in ten bucks each and buy another two. Then one of the other tables would buy the rest with other guys asking, but by then I was sold out.

I was a bootlegger and didn't even know it. Supply and demand, I called it. I justified it as a harmless service. Within a month, I was up to five cases a Sunday. These were points at twenty-four bottles per case at the cost of three dollars apiece. It was like owning a Starbucks. They lined up with cash to buy. I was blatant in my activities, but Hydro seemed to turn a blind eye. They wanted the guys happy. There were very few fights.

Though occasionally some yelling: who likes to lose their whole paycheck?

Frequently we booked the cab to town and headed to the community center and the pub before returning to camp. I had been a very good boy in camp. I'd only been in one fight, which my friends at the RCMP covered for me. In fact, that had been about competition on the bootlegging. Another young Hydro lad had followed my lead, buying bottles of whiskey and selling them. I liked free enterprise for ME!!! Not some guy pushing into my turf. I was more the monopoly type. So, I let him sell out then put my arm around him and took him outside to chat. Too many people witnessed our chat, and the RCMP was called. They determined that he started the fight and I was only defending myself. He was ejected from camp. What could he expect? Who did he think was delivering my five cases each week?

That night in town I was still pissed and was flirting with the prettiest Native American girl in the pub. I admit I was a bit on the drunk side. I was not a good drinker and didn't drink very often. This night I was loud, and she liked it. She had joined us at our table, and we were getting on just fine, I thought. About an hour into our antics she and I were talking about a room in the hotel when a local guy stomped up to our table. He told me in a drunken slur to stay away from his sister, or he would wipe my hunky ass all over Main Street. I laughed and said he'd been watching too much TV. Hunky, where did he get that? I was loud, and the crowd laughed. To my surprise, I blocked his first punch with my face.

We were outside in no time, and I went to work on this guy. I hit him so hard my hands hurt. After that first punch, he never landed another. I have fought tough guys, but he was by far the toughest. No matter what I hit him with he kept coming back. Finally, I asked him if I could buy him a pitcher of beer. He said, okay Hunky, and we both laughed.

Inside, he was drinking right from the pitcher, with blood dripping from it. His sister left with another guy. What a night.

I finally outsmarted myself. Winter was coming, and the outside work on the project would end. The crew that would stay was the indoor workers. Hydro kept about a hundred people, from engineering staff and labor, to build the generators. There was some outside work, but very little. Temperatures would drop to well below zero. The river would also freeze up with a thick blanket of ice.

The Bay had winter clothes, and I again got the idea to undersell them. Back down to Winnipeg I went and found a supplier. I bought a good supply to ship up. But, as I say, I had outsmarted myself. I made up a flyer showing the Bay's prices and mine. This got back to the Bay. I came off the night shift, went for breakfast, then to my room to sleep. A huge surprise awaited me. My suitcases were packed, and my key would not unlock the door. Then my RCMP pals showed up with the flyer. They explained that Hydro was booting me out of camp. The Bay complained and threatened to close down if I wasn't sent packing. I did make them stop at the bank for a check. I was afraid the Bay might get the money. Now I understand they couldn't, but that day I wasn't sure.

They let me say good-bye to a few friends and said they'd ship my winter clothes back to Winnipeg. Oh, and the booze was never mentioned. Honestly, I forgot to ask. I slept on the flight all the way to Winnipeg. I took a cab to Aunt Thelma's. She was always there. What a woman. It was too late to see Hersh, but I called and got to speak to him. I walked over to see Paul at the spa. To my surprise, he was in Vancouver.

I had several wonderful visits with Hersh; we did a lot of great things. It felt wonderful to have a few bucks to treat him and the other boys. I did have to apologize to the staff for my previous behavior and did that tongue in cheek. The big one said I sucker punched him or things would have been different. I offered to let him try again if it was that important to him.

I booked a trip to Hawaii and even asked if I could take Hersh. They declined. I was under age to be his temporary guardian. The JCW boss told me about a special school in Philadelphia that was equipped to handle Hersh's issues. They never shared what those issues were, only that it was the best place for him. The school, though, had an issue of its own; it was expensive. They would need a subsidy from the family to defray the costs of sending him there. The figure was around one thousand a month. He showed me the brochure. The place looked great. I called my Dad and got some BS story about why he couldn't afford it, right now. I accepted for our family and shelled out the first year in full. Hersh was excited; all looked good.

The clothes came back from the camp, but the supplier would not refund them. I took the hit and dropped them at the Salvation Army. I had a meeting with Paul, back from Vancouver, and agreed to start back at the Spa in a month, when I returned from the west. I didn't tell him that I was going to Hawaii or anything about my real estate efforts. I kissed my little brother at the airport, as he and a senior staff member boarded the plane. Then I took the red eye to Vancouver and the morning flight to Hawaii.

BACK IN OAHU, HAWAII

I could not wait to hit the waves. I had turned seventeen without a party or even a card. I took a hotel room in town and checked in with friends the next day. I had left a surfboard at my friend's mom's boat and went to collect it, then hit a small swell out front. To my surprise, my friend was in the boat. I stuck my head in, but he was forward with a woman. So, I backed out, grabbed the board, and hit the waves. About twenty minutes later, he came paddling out with a big smile on his face. He was such a great surfer; it was fun to be in the water with him.

I hooked up that night with my local realtor. Nothing had changed: he was in debt, half drunk, with a pretty lady, needed money, and had deals ready to go. I was ready to look. I wanted to build a property portfolio. It was something I'd read in a book, and it sounded good. I checked on some of the properties we had flipped. It turned out we would have made more money keeping them.

This was not his method of operation. He just wanted and needed the commission. He told me that if I held the properties longer, my capital would be tied up and wouldn't be liquid. There was something to be said for this advice. He was ready to resume our old pattern: my equity, his deals; his commission my profit. There was nothing wrong with that, except for the condos he had originally gotten me into. Their value had skyrocketed.

I wanted to have a little fun, so went out to the North Shore to reconnect with old friends. This was an eye-opening experience. These were great, wonderful, warm, loving people, but it was like I hadn't left for even a day. They hadn't changed or even moved one little bit. I, on the other hand, was different. That subdued lifestyle wasn't for and didn't suit me anymore. I wanted more for my future. I didn't know what that looked like, but I thought more money would lead the way.

If you read the original "Think and Grow Rich," the author discusses knowing the exact amount of money you want and focusing on it. The book was written in the

1930's, but the principles were sound and still hold up. I would later realize it was about accomplishment, not just in money, and it applied to anything you wanted out of life. Money was merely the medium. He was using it as a metaphor to convey his message. Since I didn't have money, and the people that had it in my view, were better than me, I concluded money was the answer.

Recent personal experience had reinforced that assessment. I now could do lots of things I'd been unable to just a few years before. I was putting my brother in a special school without help from anyone. I could stay in a nice hotel. Go on a date for dinner, and a movie like the kids in school did. Buy surfboards. Yes, I bought more than one. So, at this tender age in my life, I had committed to this path. I wasn't afraid of hard work. In fact, I welcomed and enjoyed it.

Friends had commented on how much I had changed, matured. I also could be generous and often picked up the tab. There was a bit of ego involved, I admit, mixed with satisfaction that I could. I didn't think I was rich, by any stretch of the imagination. I knew those classmates in Newport Beach, living in those mansions, and the new family I was desperately trying to adopt through my uncle's marriage, were rich. I had some money but still, couldn't show that kind of lifestyle. This adventure laid firmly planted in my mind. It was my future. I wasn't going to be denied anything and was willing to work for it all. I didn't know how but had faith that the answer would present itself along the way.

As you can see, my mastermind was very mixed. The funny thing was each group although vastly different, seem very happy and content with their position or lifestyle. It would be years while I would drill down into each group to find the other side of the picture.

Then there was my realtor; he was a piece of work. He seemed happy all the time but was always extended and living on the edge. He was fun to be around, and at the same time, you could feel he was using you for his purpose. Like a friend with benefits, I say with a smile. To this day, I have never lost on a deal with him. He always made his end, too, and many times more than me. I didn't mind that, though, until much later in our arrangement – which I had thought was a friendship.

He set up a few quick flips that were easy to fund. This put us right back on the same path. Now though, I had a little more experience under my belt and saw that these properties had greater value and potential to mold my future. They could make me as rich as the people I was striving to emulate. I started wanting to hang onto these properties and rent them out, letting the equity grow. This was the leverage lesson he'd taught me years ago.

This new attitude didn't appeal to him much. He wasn't interested in losing his finance cash cow, but he was not dumb either. So, he started making a list of good-looking solid investments. Better to make one commission than none.

THE BIG SHIFT

I liked to work and felt funny when I had nothing to do. I was spending less time in the water. I didn't care to do nothing. It felt like I was not earning in any way, and I still feel that way today. I had cash flow from the condos and could buy things. I still felt insecurity about spending. That took me a long time to overcome. I figured I had some cash in the bank and one good asset, but I didn't have a good enough plan, so I went back to the book: "Think and Grow Rich." I figured out that I was comfortable with the position in life I had created. I wasn't giving myself enough credit for how far I had come.

What did I want? I knew that I wanted to help my brother and thought I was taking care of that with the new school. I would later find out that Hersh ran away from school. He hitchhiked to the US-Canadian border. He had no ID so they called Aunty Thelma and she drove down to the border and picked him up. He gave the standard kid answer to the obvious question, "Why did you do that?" "I don't know." I spoke to him by phone. He said he liked it there but missed Aunty Thelma and Shelia. He knew what to say that loveable little bugger. What he really missed, which we all had no idea about, was drugs and smoking. He returned to the school, but two months later ran away again. Finally, the school expelled him. They intended to keep the annual fees. Eventually, they gave a partial refund to JCW, but none to me.

I rented a small apartment in town and bought my first car. It was a used, repainted, red Datsun with four doors. I had decided to do more flips, but also to look for some keepers. I was at my local breakfast spot, flipping through the newspaper ads. There was a full-page ad for "Let's Dine Out." The idea was that you would buy this card for $15.95. With it, you got two-for-one meals at twenty restaurants. There were some restrictions, mostly concerning busy hours. I thought it was a great thing for dating, which I was doing very little. I wanted to do more. One of my friends bought the card, as well.

We knew a lot of local girls, but the real fun was found in the international marketplace in the center of Waikiki. This was tourist central, and the girls were everywhere. There was a bench right in front, where we took up our position. If, and when a girl would look at us, we asked where were they were from? Same line and that was all it took. If they engaged in conversation and a boyfriend or parent didn't show up, we usually had a date. Equipped with the card, we asked if they would like to try a local dining spot. Off we would go for our 2-for-1 dinner. If we got along, we would tour them around the island. Normally, they were there for between three to five days if touring the entire island chain, or a week to two weeks if only visiting Waikiki. The point is, I had a lot of dates. Yes, I went through three of those cards. The staff at the restaurants got to know me. I asked how effective the card was. It turns out it was very effective: some said it had become their only source of advertising. They considered the free meal advertising expenditures. My friend and the girls just wanted to get back to either their hotel or my apartment and continue the party, but this interested me, and I wanted to know more.

A few days later I went down to the local office posing as a new restaurant owner wanting to know how the program worked. The office girl was very helpful, and I left with everything including their contract. The card they used was business card quality, with numbers around the outside for the restaurants to punch their number. There was a list of the spots, by address and phone number, with any restrictions. They signed the restaurant up for one year. The card was good for the calendar year. The card company did their big advertising push in the month of January, with full-page ads in the local paper. By March they just had the office staffed with this girl. The owners were from California and returned to sign up the next year's restaurants. The card didn't have the client's name on it; anyone that possessed it could use it. The girl said that they sold fifty thousand cards in January. They brought in just under eight hundred thousand dollars in one month. Ten thousand more sold throughout the year with guys like me buying a second card. I did the math, almost a million bucks a year with the operation cost of the ads in January, some print material, and a plastic-coated business card.

It was all marketing, and I had an idea to improve on it. I had eaten at all the restaurants on their list. I asked the owners how they felt about the program and if another card came along would they participate? They all were affirmative. I started my research on the hybrid I had an idea to develop.

Several of us surfers made our own boards. We got most of the materials from the mainland and had them shipped over. Some of the guys sold the boards and had a little business. Others just wanted their own design. I wasn't very skilled at this, but it was fun to be involved and have my friend's design boards that they thought suited my skill level. Since we had all surfed together for years, we knew each other's style.

My idea was to form a buying group and purchase the blanks and other materials together, getting some volume discounts.

The guys liked the idea. My friend and I flew to the mainland and met the suppliers. We got the best volume deals that many of the shops were getting. I placed orders and paid up front. They helped with the shipping as they had contracts in place.

Back on the island, we showed the guys the savings. Some were huge. One of the guys had a car sound system shop and said we could all have a discount with him. Another owned a clothing store and offered the same. Then I asked them if they knew the "Let's Dine Out" program? Two of them had the card. I was doing market research and didn't even know.

I had the card company's contract so I used that to make up my own. I was going to call my venture "UniSurf United We Stand." I incorporated my first company. My realtor introduced me to a lawyer. He wanted to be my partner after I ran my idea past him. I didn't answer, and eventually, we dropped the subject.

The realtor was showing me several deals, most of them were flips in his mind, but now with a little twist, renovations. He suggested we buy old, cheap properties and have them fixed up. He was looking in Pearl City and other military areas. We tried one. We bought it way under market from an officer transferring back to the mainland. He just wanted out of the property. We repainted it and put in new fixtures and appliances. The place looked great. This time my realtor would put his commissions into the property and participate as my partner. It was still my property at risk. He had all the right connections and arranged all the construction contractors, almost always local guys. I didn't have to do a lot, but I liked showing up in the morning when they started work and dropping by at the close of the day.

Next, I would go off and see retailers and restaurant owners recruiting for my new business. I wanted to expand the dining to discounts at one hundred locations. You could dine at two-for-one, like my competitor, and get discounts of ten to twenty percent on a wide assortment of products, ranging from clothing to furniture, musical instruments, and lessons, to surfboards. I could even provide tourist adventures at a discount. My card's price was going to be the same, $15.95 each, but offer so much more. Also, the membership would be one year from the date you signed up, so I could sell all year. Their card started losing value towards the end of the year, approaching the December expiration date. If you didn't use it up, you lost out. Their office girl, who I was dating now, told me that by September sales dropped. Of course, I missed the fact that their program was based on the one-month membership push.

Meanwhile, we had four renovations on the go. I liked this and felt like we were doing something good by taking these old, run down properties and making them look brand new. The money was good, too.

I gave my card vendors the choice to track their discounts and receive the figures at the end of the year. They could then deduct them as an advertising expense. For that service, I charged them one hundred dollars. I created an administrative nightmare for myself, though I hadn't realized it at the time. I was going on what one of the first restaurant owners had told me about using the program as his source of advertising. I played on that in my presentation to the other vendors. Most of them took the hundred-dollar package. They were reluctant to pay right away as the program was going to kick off next year. I said I would bill them in the first quarter. I also had to figure out how to keep track of their numbers.

I had orange, plastic cards made, with the logo embossed in gold. The client's name would be typed on them, also embossed in gold. I ordered ten thousand cards for my first year. I bought equipment for printing the name on the card and embossing it with the gold. This was cool. But I created more labor for myself, again. These were rookie business mistakes that I would pay for later.

Then, in the real estate business, my now, partner found the big deal. It was a 120-unit apartment building, with a mix of one and two bedrooms across the street from the beach. Wow! I wanted it.

MY NEW APARTMENT COMPLEX

There were a few things that led up to this purchase, teaching some big lessons. Initially, I listened to my realtor friend, as he was my mentor. My trust of him though soon revealed how naive and unsophisticated I was.

This was a gigantic purchase for me. I wanted it very badly. I experienced the market movement for years, so I was confident of the outcome. I didn't want to flip, though. I wanted to own and operate the property. This apartment block and its condos were going to be my asset base. My new business was going to be my cash flow. Napoleon Hill would have been proud of me.

We made an offer on the building, but I needed money for the down payment. I was instructed to form a company to receive the asset and not place it in my personal name. I didn't totally understand the reasoning for this but followed the advice of those I trusted. My realtor friend and the owner went back and forth until a price was struck. It had several subjects, which were quite standard. I would see them over and over during my career. In addition, there was the finance package. This was a big deal. Because of my age, many banks wanted twenty-five per cent down. I didn't have that. I was thinking ten per cent, as with the other properties.

I knew I could make the payment. The building was full, and I had the additional rental income from the condos. There were some problems, though. First, those properties were lodged as collateral against our renovation projects. The bank we settled on wanted certain information to structure the loan. All I wanted to do was close the deal. Again, this was inexperience creeping into my behavior. I felt they should just trust me. Have you stopped laughing? At that time, I thought banks were here to help. Silly me.

There was also the question of the down payment. My realtor suggested I sell one more condo. It would sell quickly and provide most of what I needed. The profit from the renovation projects would easily bring in the rest. Security would be provided from the rest of the condos and their income. There was one small problem, though. I had a charge on them with a finance company at much higher than normal interest rates. I was also informed that I had over secured the loans by an unreasonable amount. I had never thoroughly checked it. My realtor friend had handled it, and I simply went in to sign. It hadn't mattered to me that they weren't a bank. They'd fronted all the money, on time, and we made a profit.

You might see where this was going. The banker showed me what he could do and how much he could save me. It was substantial. He would take out my current loan and take over the charge using that as security for my mortgage. All I needed to do was pay the down payment and get them a record of the rental income, and with that, I was approved.

We had the condo listed, and offers came in quickly. My realtor suggested we accept one with a quick closing. I now had the down payment covered. All I needed then were the records required by the bank. I went to the hotel and asked for the payment records. They were happy to help. Their records showed they had been making payments to another company, not part of their rental pool.

The renovations were also concluding. I still visited every morning. I liked the guys and we all "talked shit," a Hawaiian term for chatting. The contractor was from San Diego. He was fun to talk with and, most importantly, did excellent work, on time. This day he had the bills for the last two jobs and asked me to pass them on to my realtor. Since the bills landed on my desk for payment, anyway, I took them. When I got home, I opened them. I discovered that this was the same company paying me the rent from the condos. I was confused and returned to the bank with all my records. The manager, a Hawaiian, was most helpful in unraveling the mess, to my resulting dismay.

It turned out I had been a victim of this realtor for years. I didn't want to believe it. This just couldn't be! I felt like a mule kicked me in the gut. In black and white, the rental record from the hotel revealed, in no uncertain terms, that he had been dipping into the rent from the start. Then, comparing my files with the contractor's, we found he had done the same with each renovation bill he presented me. Going back through all the flips, it turned out that all the bills were padded with payments to this company. I never noticed. I just signed off and took my profit. This was such a shock that the man I trusted the most and had helped so much would do this. At this point, he didn't know I had any idea of what he'd been doing. It was funny since my usual reaction would have been to find a dark alley and have a go at him.

I was plenty mad and wanted revenge, but I needed advice. Who could I go to? First, I felt stupid that anyone would know I let this happen to me. Second, I knew this guy's lifestyle. He wouldn't have anywhere near enough to repay. He was already talking about how much he needed the commission from this apartment deal to clear some debts.

When I moved the monthly rental income from this company to my new company, he would know, though. Also, he'd know I knew, when the bank paid out the finance company for the loans on the renovation business. The titles were in my name and could be transferred to my new company. I decided to keep all four properties. The contractor also informed me that it was he who'd brought the four renovation deals to my realtor and he had others that he would like to partner on.

I called two people: Uncle Chuck and Uncle Blackie. Chuck told me to chop this guy into little pieces and feed him to the sharks. That did sound good. Blackie asked if there was any way to get my money back. My banker had some suggestions, as well. He was local and had connections. My realtor did not have a very good reputation among the Islanders. In fact, it was quite the opposite.

We had deals concluding, and he was expecting his cut. Maybe, just maybe, I could recoup something. I asked if he wanted to be a partner in both the card business and the apartments. He said, "Of course," and that was the plan. He went on to explain that we could use the same rental pool company to manage the building and collect the rent. After all, they had been doing such a nice job. Playing dumb, I said," I thought it was just for the hotel?" He was quick to say they had a division just for this and did a lot of building management in town. He was quick; I will give him that. He said the charges were well below market and that was why they had so much business. Many of his clients used them. That sounded like we needed to do the same, I said.

I pointed out that he would need about one hundred thousand, in addition to his commission, to secure his percentage of the apartments. Also, there was an additional forty thousand to get in the card deal. I'd just made that up. He tried to get around the hundred thousand as a loan from me, but I told him I was too extended with the bank. He suggested we sell another condo. I said the bank had them as part of the loan. I pointed out, though, that we were going make money right away with the card business so that he would have plenty of cash. Plus, we were going to be positive in the apartment, with the management in place, all we had to do was collect. Then, I said, we could do some more flips, using this contractor who did such good work. If the market was going up, as he said, we'd be good!

I thought I knew where he would go for his short-term loan. I had been to this scary side of the island before with him when he'd paid off these guys. I didn't even want to get out of the car.

We left it that he would get his money in two days and sign over the commission on the apartment deal. He could draft up some sort of note to give to the lawyers later. The emphasis was on just getting this deal closed quickly. We only had a week left on the extension that the owner was nice enough to give us after talking to our banker.

He brought the check and a letter, with all kinds of stuff protecting him. I just picked up the pen and signed both copies. He said we would draw up something formal, but for now, this would do. He even drove me to the bank to deposit it. Then, we went for a beer to celebrate our big deal.

It was going to be a short celebration for him.

The deal closed and shit hit the fan hard. He came to me about the finance company being taken out. As you could guess, he had been getting points on the commission. He didn't have that arrangement with the bank and interest went down dramatically. Then, the rental pool fraud was exposed. When he didn't get his monthly rental payment from the hotel, he was back at me. I just said I found a better company for less money; he should be happy that they agreed to handle the apartments, too. What could he say? He did try to argue that we had a contract with them and they might sue us. Oh, I explained, I am going to keep the renovation properties and rent them out. But, he proposed, "I have buyers for them." I didn't know that, but no worries: the contractor had more properties he wanted us to back him on. So, there would be commissions for him, in and out of them, if I had the credit to handle it.

He went out on the lanai to smoke. When he returned, I switched the conversation to the card company and all my plans. I confess I wanted to throw him off the lanai. I only lived on the second floor, though. It wasn't nearly high enough.

The deal closed and he was exposed. He had borrowed the money from the wrong guys. That was the last I heard of him for years. We did an accounting of what was stolen; it was a great deal more than was recovered. He did promise to pay it back and even signed a note.

The bank helped me set up the collection for the rent. I hired a young Chinese girl, an accounting student, to come in part time for bookkeeping and accounts payable. Then, I hired an ex-military sergeant as a property manager, after I had a go at it. He could just about do any job that came up and lived on site for a rent discount as pay.

I took an apartment in the complex: first a one bedroom, to save money. Then I upgraded to a two bedroom, on the top floor, when it came available. I converted the second bedroom into office space. Then, I expanded to the kitchen and living room as needed when I started the card company.

UNISURF UNITED WE STAND

This was a fun training stage for my future retail, and much of my marketing, education. We all tend to have our go-to areas, depending on our educational experiences and comfort. I had the manure and the real estate businesses as my marketing training. For the rest, I followed what others were doing. It was not a perfect or easy road. I made many mistakes but usually covered them with hard work and cash flow.

I did think I had a better plan than "Let's Dine Out." Although, later, I appreciated the simple genius of their marketing approach. I thought I was expanding that approach, generating broader card usage and better value. I didn't appreciate the challenges of sharing that message, so people knew about the value. Also, there was the question of the money collection. They received everything in one location. People either mailed a check or called with a credit card. During their first two months, in conjunction with their advertising campaign, they had a full phone staff. Many people were brought over from the mainland. Then, they trimmed the office staff down to just two, then one operator, for reorders or late buyers.

I had a good concept, but a poor business plan. It all seemed logical, and even practical, but it was not going to work functionally. My biggest mistake was wanting to employ a sales force, like the manure business. I would pay them commission each day when they brought their sales to the office. I figured that I could do a better job without the ads.

The first month was a disaster. Everything went wrong. My sales staff was guys from the beach, and they all needed money. I was training at my apartment, with donuts, juice, and coffee. They wiped me out of food. That should have been a clue. But, no, I plunged forward. We had sign-up paperwork, with a list of our merchants and restaurants. Cardholders paid by cash or check before we sent out the cards. They did look sharp. We had samples to show people.

We were going door to door, again, just like the manure business. People in Hawaii, though, didn't like solicitation, so we made few sales. Just as bad, for some sales, if they were in cash, sometimes I never saw money or the sales member, either. This created two problems. One was that I didn't know who was buying, so I couldn't send them the card. The other problem was that the cash was gone. And of course, I didn't even know what I didn't know. Some of the clients called to ask where their card was. They, of course, were not on the list. Sometimes, I had the staff still with me, and I found out they were stealing.

In call cases, when I got such a complaint, I made up a card and hand delivered it, eating the loss. The first month's sales were 232 cards, with 70 of them sold by me. After commissions...I don't even want to share with you the losses it would just make me cry, or, actually, laugh!!!!!

Remember the girl I was dating from the other card company? She informed me they sold $37,000-plus in the first two weeks. Ok, it wasn't exactly the competitive race I had hoped would win me market domination. But, I had a new plan.

There was a lag time between the sale and the card deliveries. (The cards I knew about.) I didn't know how many people I'd inadvertently ripped off with my shiftless sales force. If I found out, I corrected it, but I am sure and sorry to say, some people just forgot about it. There had to be a better way.

I called my entire customer base. That was something my competitor couldn't, and didn't do. I asked if they had used the card and thanked them for joining. I also asked if there were other services they might suggest including.

This was a great investment of my time and effort. Most were happy to talk to me and shared their views openly. One of the best inputs was suggesting the use of credit cards to buy the membership. I didn't want to do that, in those days the bank charged 5% on each purchase and one dollar service charge under twenty dollars. I was subject to that charge. I went to see my banker, who was sympathetic, but unwilling to help. Since I had heard the same thing so many times from my clients, I took the bank service. In those days, you just had to get the credit card number, and you could process. Later, you had to copy the card.

The one encouraging insight from the follow-up calls was that they were using the card. Some had also bought the other card. This wasn't what I wanted to hear, but it was helpful input. They said I had a bigger selection of restaurants and the other products were a bonus. Some had gotten the retail discounts and informed me they'd paid for the card. In turn, a few of my retailers took the $100 account package. We settled on them using a credit card slip, which they gave them for free. I picked up the slips, totaled them, and send out the report so that they could deduct the discounts as advertising. This was cool; getting a $100 check. Here I am with my real estate business, financing this little venture, and I got excited about a hundred bucks. I was living in the moment.

This was a challenge, but I was up to the task of making it work, somehow. First, obviously, I needed a better plan. Then, I needed to stop being the boss and get my ass out in the field see what worked, instead of relying on others telling me. I had to see for myself.

The second thing I addressed was my promotional approach. My new log line was, "Get Your Card for Free." The new brochure emphasized that two dinners paid off the cost of the card. Real testimonials from members described saving almost $1000 at a club furniture store.

The third thing to address was the lag time between sign-up and the card's arrival. I printed two-week temporary cards that we dated as we sold them. This way the customers could start enjoying the benefits that day. If you didn't get your card before the temporary one expired, we delivered it to your home.

Then, I started controlling the number of cards the sales staff had. They had to sell them or return them. Either way, I now had a full accounting. I held back commissions one week, ensuring the staff stuck around to get paid. If they left before the week was up, as some did, I kept the commissions. At least, now, I knew within a day whether I was being cheated

I went into the field and tried different sales methods. I found a simple approach. "Would you like to Save Money TODAY!" I followed that with an explanation of the program. Mall entrances worked best. That approach was especially effective at those malls where we had a few of our merchants located. I produced a classy sign, like Visa's, for the merchant's windows and doors. I brought my crew to three or four places a day, and we started selling. At first, we sold 20-30 cards a day; then it was over a hundred. I set up each location, then moved between them all day. One day, a salesperson sold one hundred cards, making over $5000.

Administration and card production and circulation were the next challenges. By now I had two girls in the office, where I dropped off the cards, three times a day.

I had a part timer in at night. In the morning, I posted them on my way to setting up the first location. We started setting up a table at youth sporting events. That worked very well.

One of my merchants was an elder at a large church. We gave the preacher a free card. He hit up the group and sold nine hundred cards, receiving five dollars each for the church and one dollar each for the merchant. She didn't donate that. I didn't care. The preacher recommended me to three other churches. Those referrals resulted in many sales and an override to him. It became a fundraiser, with huge benefits to the new card members.

My new brochures had more testimonials. And, the pitch got even simpler. Same lead line, then, "It works." Next, there was one testimonial after another. On the back, were the merchant listings. Next, I put "join our sales team" and listed some incomes. We had merchants that allowed us to set up tables in their stores to sell our cards. We offered them overrides, but most of them did it for free. We were bringing in new customers and, with the card, they would keep coming back.

As result of this success, I had to order twenty thousand new blank membership cards. We almost sold out the first ten thousand in three months. There were two men and a woman who developed into my sales leaders. I created a competition between them: they got a one dollar override on their crews' sales and an additional six dollars on their personal sales. To qualify for the override, they had to be the number one sales person in their crew for the week. Then, I created a pot of an additional one dollar from all the sales of the three crews. The number one crew's chief won that amount each week. It was a significant amount of money. Many weeks, over four thousand cards were sold. This kind of money attracted better people and created more competition. Soon, I had six crew chiefs and established first, second, and third place prize bonuses. In April, I ordered thirty thousand new cards for close to the same price that I had bought the first ten thousand. The longer the run, the cheaper was the price. It was the same with printing too. I was learning, but I lost sight of the bottom line. With real estate, I was always in the black. But with this business, I found that I was giving away most of my profit. This became clear when I got my first P&L (Profit and Loss statement).

Looking at my results, my members were happy, my merchants were happy, and my sales staff was super happy. My office staff was paid, and I think they were happy? Then there I was, making less than a dollar a card profit. Not so happy. I was cash short at times and had to dip into my savings or other cash streams. Thank god I had them. I was only working 18-20 hours a day, seven days a week. I would cat nap either in the other bedroom at the home office or down by the pool. And I couldn't remember the last time I had surfed – or even saw my friends. I had this deep feeling of accomplishment. I did have over thirty thousand members that were for the most part, happy. We had very few complaints, and those few were about the service received from a merchant. Those we just forwarded, asking the merchant to contact the member and make it right. For the most part, they were happy to do so: it was a win-win for all concerned. In many of those cases, they offered some type of added value, like a free dinner or cocktails. If the member was still disenchanted, I would offer to refund the membership. This only happened twice. In one case, they were so mad they yelled at my office girl and made her cry. I took the phone and blasted them, letting them know I knew where they lived. We just sent them a check that day. The funny thing is, if they kept using the card, we had no way of knowing. We weren't computerized. We had no way at all of checking, but it felt good.

Summer was approaching and I was missing Hersh. It was our birthdays in May. I asked JCW if I could take him on vacation. I was turning nineteen, and he was ten. They agreed. I didn't tell them where we planned to go; Disneyland!!! We had a ball. We visited all the relatives and went down to my old surfing beaches. I even put him on a surfboard. He didn't like the ocean, much, though. Occasionally, he would go off for a walk and return smelling like smoke. He would just say there were people around him smoking. It was funny how those people were always around. I hated smoking, and this would be an issue between us until he quit on his own many years later.

We had such a great time, and I cried for two days when I dropped him off at the home. I did a petition for his release to me. They took it as far as requiring me to provide financial statements showing my ability to care for him. In the end, though, they rejected my request on the grounds of my age and location. My uncle thought I lied on my statements. He did say he didn't blame me and would have backed me if I needed help. My dad later said he was asked what he thought and he told them he didn't think Hersh was better off with me.

Back in Winnipeg, Paul hired me again, this time as a salesperson. There was only one of the old staff left. The district manager Henry P. was coming to town, so we had a super cleaning. Henry wore hundred dollar shoes and dressed extremely sharp. I didn't know him but wanted to impress him. We were pushing for upgrades to lifetime memberships. It was $480. The good thing about it was that Paul had to sign off on it. He was in one of the closing offices meeting with Henry after they toured the facility, which we got a glowing review. I had a plan. I signed everyone that walked through the door to the lifetime membership. I interrupted them nine times for Paul to sign off for me. Finally, Henry said, is this the guy that knows our manual word for word? Paul was glowing as he answered, "Yes". Henry tested me on the only section he knew. I passed. There was something in the wind about a move to New York, but it was never mentioned to me. At least, until I told Paul I had to return to Hawaii.

BACK IN HAWAII

I left the number one sales lady in charge of the crews, and I got reports each week. She was doing a good job. The office was running a little slow, but I was betting they would be current as soon as they heard I was coming home.

My building manager was a gem and acted as my eyes on the renovation jobs. He had a few bucks saved and wanted to invest. I didn't need his money. I did figure he'd be even more attentive with his own money in the game. Oh, and, the contractor was taking a piece of each deal, too. He offered a net deal, and he threw in cash as well. We were knocking off two or three renovations every quarter. There was a nice Hawaiian lady realtor that came through the contactor. She wasn't a daimyo, but she got the job done.

I arrived to find things in pretty good shape. I was about to catch a great break. There was a radio personality, turned TV host with a daytime show on the largest local network. He did local pieces, about the community, restaurant reviews, Hawaiian style cooking, entertainment reviews, even surfing reports, when a big swell hit. He was very popular on both his radio and TV show. His staff called me about the card. His friend was a member, and he wanted to interview me on TV. I had never done anything like that before. I must say, I was tremendously nervous.

I was at the station sitting in the waiting room when a girl came to get me. She asked me to sit in a chair and wanted to put makeup on me. I stopped her.

This guy's stage name was Granny Goose. He came in and said he didn't like the makeup either, but it's for the bright lighting. He took me into the studio. It was nothing as it looked on TV. He was a cool guy and made me feel immediately comfortable. He was easy to talk to, as well. He went over the list of merchants with an eye to consuming from them. He even suggested some nightclubs with two-for-one drinks and show tickets.

A few days later I was invited to do a radio show with him. He told me they got a lot of good feedback with people calling the station asking where they could sign up. Then he suggested advertising on both the radio and TV. I didn't think I had the budget for it, so he suggested going in some of my bigger merchants. He would be our spokesman. It was an endorsement deal. I called some merchants and, to my surprise, they were game.

This was a wow for me. When I got three merchants to cooperate, and my costs were zero. Granny would talk about using the card with them and how much he saved. Also, we started a contest and the person that saved the most money each quarter got a trip to Las Vegas. Granny got Hawaiian Airlines to sponsor it and a hotel to throw in the room, food, and beverages. He told me, with my list of advertisers (my merchants), I was pure gold to him. What an education in advertising.

My card sales doubled, then tripled. We were close to fifty thousand members, now. My profits were picking up from all the people joining without needing to pay any sales commission. The sale efforts were growing exponentially, too. We could now do sign up days at the merchants. During their sales, they advertised through the co-op. Granny would promote them and come on location. If you signed up there, you got an additional discount on your day's purchase. In some cases, people saved the membership price right on-the-spot and Granny would make a big deal out of it.

I brought pretty surfer girls to these events and paid them by the hour. So, again, there were better margins on the card. People were signing up without a pitch. The sales presentation the girls used just explained how to use the card and provided a list of merchants. We could sign up four hundred to a thousand on a weekend.

My real payday was the first-year renewals, commission-free. We had a system: two months before your card expired you got a free drink with meals at all our bars, lounges, and restaurants. The deal was that most people ordered another drink. Also, many paid the renewal by check to qualify for a bonus. That cut out the credit card commission. I also raised the fee to

$19.95. No one complained; they understood the value.

Two years later I sold the membership to a swimwear company, as I was spending most of my time in New York, working with Paul and his partner Bob.

HELLO BIG APPLE

I had moved to Vancouver that year. My girlfriend wanted to start a Health Food business. I was going to New York and could only finance her share. She was going to have a partner, but at the last minute he crapped out, so I put up all the money. It is a long story, and I will get to back to that because it becomes one of my core businesses, which provided me the cash to grow.

Paul and Bob had bought the rights to a company called Nu Dimensions. This was figure salons, for women only. Bob was getting New York and his other partner in the Spa business, Ray, was going to Chicago. Paul was Bob's mentee, and now I was Paul's.

I was offered a contract that I would own 25% of all my salons Bob 50% and Paul 25%. Paul would also run salons 50-50 with Bob.

I asked Uncle Chuck to look it over, and he referred me to Uncle Blackie. We were all having dinner at Blackie's beautiful apartment. He took me upstairs to his bedroom office for some privacy. He read the contract, and his exact words were "Arie, this is a shit load of money." He called his brother Abe, the family lawyer and a QC (Queen's Council). He made a few suggestions to which Paul and Bob agreed.

While still in Winnipeg, Paul informed me I'd need a suit. I had a light blue pin-striped one made at a Jewish tailor that my uncle recommended. I didn't know Bob very well, but he was Mr. Big; a multimillionaire. I was so impressed with him and them for that matter. I must say, these men played as hard as they worked. They would both teach me great lessons about what to do, and also what not to do, which can be just a valuable.

Paul had told me when traveling, go first class and stay in a hotel suite. I did just that, without question, until years later, when I stopped wasting money on suites when I was alone. Oh, and, let me tell you, I would take my money out for a spin with great intensity.

My first-class Air Canada flight landed at JFK airport in the evening. Paul was not there to greet me. I was paged to pick up a courtesy phone. It was Paul, sounding a little curt. These men, as I would discover, hit the liquor cabinet as hard as I have ever seen. Away, I went to the taxi stand. My first experience was a businessman asking if I were going into Manhattan and if I wanted to share a cab. The cabby tried to charge us each the meter price and my new friend went off on him. Sure, this cabbie was trying to rip us off. When my friend got out first, he made the cabbie reset the meter for the ride to my hotel. I just watched. We exchanged contact information, and he said he'd call me.

The cab rolled up to the Summit of New York, at Fifty-First and Lexington. The street was busy. The doormen pulled out the luggage, and I was suddenly at the front desk. Again, Paul called this time to inform me they were held up at a meeting, although I heard music and a crowd in the background. He was a little less coherent than during the first call. I was shown to a penthouse, two-bedroom suite. Wow! This was luxury unlike I had ever seen before. There was a large parlor with a dining table, two couches, four armchairs and a bar. On each side of the sitting room was a bedroom. Paul called the room and told me I would be in the parlor and that two bottles of Champagne were being sent up so I should sign for them. I explored both bedrooms. Each had king size beds and a sitting area, with couch and chair, and a desk. In Bob's bathroom was all cologne, "Kanon." Boy, I liked that scent. So, this was what multimillionaires wear. I wanted to splash some on, but I was afraid he'd smell it on me and know I was snooping - which of course I was.

It was late, and I made up one of the couches. It was a fold out. I was asleep maybe an hour when the door burst open, all the lights go on, and they're home. Not thinking they had company, I bounced out of bed to get my clothes and found two girls sitting on them. I usually don't wear my underwear to bed, but fortunately had this night. It was one of those moments you just don't forget. I was banished to Paul's bedroom, while they continued their party. Then banished back when he wanted his room.

In the morning, they started with a loud noise, motivating their start to the day. We were all football players. They liked the raw-raw just like me, so I fit right in. There was a line of mentorship. Above Bob was Ray, who was huge. Later in my career, I met him. Bob had Paul and, now, Paul had me. Bob made himself available to me more and more as he got to know me and my abilities. I liked him. Though he was tough and you didn't want to be on his bad side. These men's management style was all about control. I learned that from them but found out eventually it just didn't work. You couldn't create independent people by jumping all over them. That turned out to be one of the greatest lessons I learned in my business career and in life. A good method of operation was, If you hire a person for a job, make sure they know what you want them to do, and then let them do it. Though still checking to ensure you'd trained them properly. If so, though, let them do their job. I'll come back to this: it explains how I held myself back, for years.

Management and the development of people will make or break you if your desire is to be larger than you can control yourself in one day. Like expanding to a new location and it doesn't do as good as the one you manage. Getting the most out of people is a real skill and can be learned. I picked up a lot of what not to do from these partners.

My experiences in New York matured me as a young businessman. I had opportunities to develop many skills on my own, as they couldn't lead where they didn't know where they were going. I never understood their direction or the outcome they desired. When I left them, it was for very specific reasons, and I felt even as their junior, they were short sighted.

One of the biggest things they did was to bring on a think tank; brilliant guys from MIT and Harvard. We had hit the market very hard. They had massive advertising budgets and aggressive expansion of locations. Bob brought in some of the old people from the spa business, many of which had gone on to other business. A few were family members. Paul also recruited from the spa industry. I got to know most of them as it was me who developed the training program.

The thing was I was in the field selling and working with the members we were signing up. I had the day-to-day skills to run a location. I had my checkpoints in place to solve problems fast. Paul was at the corporate office, which was in a location where he and Bob had big beautiful offices.

That location, in my opinion, should have been the training center and Paul should have been more active. I didn't like the fact that their focus was always around getting the gross. Get the gross, what are your numbers for the day. Yes, sales were our profit center, but it was our only profit center, and our clients were consuming middle-aged women. We were not taking advantage of the additional profit all around use.

I brought this up several times to get laughed out of the room for talking nickels and dimes as they mocked me. The think tank liked my ideas and even encouraged me to try some in my own locations. Remember, I have two businesses that are selling small ticket items, the Card and the Vitamin companies.

These think tank guys also showed me Wall Street and to them, I opened up about my other assets. They were amazed and wondered why I even bothered with Bob and Paul. This was again Napoleon Hill; find the people when you need the people. I never knew the contract Bob had with this group. They did come up with incredible control sheets for our location reporting system. I know, as I used them daily and the information I needed to run my locations was right there. I have used those systems in many other businesses and created hybrids for others.

In short, there was just very little creativity in our management team. They did things the way they did them before, with hammer force. Even after I had broken all the sales records in Winnipeg the first time I worked for Paul, he saw the result but not the change in thinking. He missed the point. In New York, it was the same thing. His locations were not doing nearly as well as mine. I would train up staff; then he would transfer them to his locations. When he brought in people from other spas, he would put them with me for training.

I was a team player and still looked up to Paul. I spent time with his family, and he treated me the way Bob treated him. I wasn't the big drinker, but I didn't mind it. He spent many a night on my couch too drunk drive home. So did Bob for that matter.

I want to step over all the negative issues I had in New York, as there were many positives. I loved the city. I learned so much; so many rich lessons. I loved live theater. A young aspiring actress that I was dating introduced me to Broadway. I became a huge fan and still am today. There was so much to do in the big apple. My focus was money even though I had some it wasn't enough.

The straw that broke the camel's back was another lesson I would learn from Paul and Bob. As we grew, there entered a powerful businessman, Jim. He was involved with public companies and was a million dollar round table insurance salesperson. He had a mover and a shaker attitude. I liked being around him, and it seemed he enjoyed my questions. He also filled in the blanks about Bob's fortune. Bob had an interest in the finance company that bought the sales contracts from the spas. Ray, his mentor, had started this company and Bob was a minor interest. They took it public, or something like that, and Bob cashed in. He also shared Paul's story, which was not as fruitful. Deep inside, I felt to beware of false profits. I was in a better position than all of them, and I didn't know it. Jim left after he saw the mess they were making. The public company now owned the spas, all but Winnipeg's four locations that would become part of the deal with Bob.

Okay back to that straw. Bob had started a finance company with Ray to buy the contracts from our locations. They factored our paper for a thirty per cent discount. Our customers would sign a promissory note that gave permission for this to happen and they would be called just as in Winnipeg to confirm their understanding. If you didn't pay, you would be sued. I had to in New York go to court several times and testify as to our sales presentation.

If the finance company disproved the credit application, they would put it in their file two sections. They would then pay out use each month less their thirty percent. So, they don't take any risk. In Winnipeg, they would pay out the commission on all sales after the verification call was done. We would even tell our clients they would be getting the call. If they turned it down the contact would come back to us.

Here was the huge issue. In New York, they started out doing the same thing as I was used to in Winnipeg. I was the top salesperson in the company by miles. They had a, win a trip incentive, for the top sales person. They ran that promotion for a year. I won every month. The joke around the company was I would have to take a year off to collect my prizes, and then they could make some money. I suggested to Paul that he make a different promotion, but I guess he felt that one was good. I asked for cash instead but was refused, so I started using the trips in my locations for my staff. I was making 10% on my own sales and a 5% override on my salons of which I had six. This was bringing me in some hefty coin, which I was plowing back into real estate.

Late one evening Bob and Paul visited me at the location I was training a new manager. I have always felt the speed of the leader was the speed of the pack. I worked the floor and did sales and helped them close sales splitting the commission no free lunch. They learned to call on me only when they needed me. My staff was well trained.

The last staff member said good night and Bob started in on me. He had a printout of my last quarter's sales. He began with the fact that he felt I was signing up junk. These people are all credit risks, and we can't sell the paper. We are going to have to implement a chargeback program. He then explained how it was going to work.

All sales that were filed two papers will have the commissions charged back starting forthwith.

"Are you kidding me?" I asked. "No and yours is pretty steep," he informed me. In his pocket, he has the checks for all my sales staff and myself. I am shown the figures. Holy crap some of my people won't get a check and will, in fact, owe more out of their next check.

"Bob, you know the people need their money; they worked for it, earned it. If you implement this policy, we are going to lose possibly all of them. This is crazy. Then he pulled out another spreadsheet; this one is just me. My people get their checks and start the new system next month. I eat both their chargebacks and mine. The logic here I am just not getting. I am pulling down 25- 40 grand a month. It is going to take me 3-4 months to break even. We have a new super location opening in Forest Hills, a prime location in my territory. They play that card as a high-income area, which it is, and if I do most the selling, I will need top dollar again. I did ask Paul what he thought, and he sided with Bob.

Well, I couldn't have my sale staff subjected to this shit, so I said to make their checks up, and I want to talk to you again. Bob said he would do that, but the discussion was closed. I later called one of the Think Tank Melt that I had bonded with and asked for advice. He said he would talk to the guys and get back to me. When he did, it was good news. They had spoken to the powers, Bob and Paul. It was suggested that they would have almost destroyed the moral of their strongest arm; me. He informed me that they were cash short and just felt they could bully me.

Eventually, I did get paid out, but I had to remind them many times. Melt, my new situation with real estate offered me some alternatives. He said that there was a ton of capital in Switzerland, that his group was using. He had contacts that might be interested in the property. He explained that everyone in his group did investing. Over the next few months, I got to know them all pretty well. They had beautiful apartments, nice cars, and toys and yet they were easy to talk with.

I showed them my other investments, and they seemed impressed. Funny, because I felt the other way. Really, they were more like big brothers, like the way I once felt about Paul. The day he left me hanging when Bob hung me out to dry distanced me from him. That, as I looked back, was the beginning of the end in my mind. I could, and in my entire career would never do that to anyone much less an employee.

My friendship with these geniuses came with multiple benefits. They realized I had little formal education and recommended books I should read. When I reported that I was having problems reading through the list fast enough they tested me. What we did find was I suffered from severe dyslexia. Man, the bells went off in my head. All these years I thought I was stupid. There were more tests they helped me find that uncovered my disability. My left eye and my brain are not in sync. This throws my right eye off well as my reading. That is why when I use my finger to go word by word, I get it, but the process is very slow. Wow, I am in my second year with Paul and Bob, and I have this breakthrough.

I admit I was becoming a different person. I changed my learning process to pictures and audio. I started attending seminars all the time. Some they recommended, some I found myself. It is nice to find out you are not stupid. They pointed out what I had accomplished. They said that most of their brethren from Harvard and MIT had not done nearly as well. They were actually complimenting me. I can't tell you what this did for my self-esteem. I had been complimented before by my teacher in that gifted kid's class, but she abandoned me like all the people I trusted. I would later find that was a core issue and I needed to deal with it. I did, but later than sooner.

I know I am spending a great deal of time on this chapter, but it was a true pinnacle in my life that opened some new doors. This was speaking volumes to Faith again from Hill's writings. There was so much growth in these short years.

I must share where this took me. Melt took me to meet the investment bankers. They liked the idea of Hawaii property and were interested in financing my purchase if the structure was right, and I could provide them with the proper security. I showed them where the market had gone, and what I held now. We devised a plan for under which I could operate.

We opened the big salon in Forest Hills, and it was a huge success. Paul was bringing in burned out spa people from Toronto, Canada. I was to train them, and I refused. He would just take them away from me and waste my time. I also was doing things in my salon that the chain didn't do. This made me unique, and I learned that is a key to all business.

I had my exit strategy planned and didn't know it. Bob had brought his niece in from Vancouver to learn the business. She was something; not only beautiful but a wonderful person. I met her parents, they too were great. They were working class people. The Dad ran a business that cleaned the Vancouver spas that Bob's now public company owned. Bob owned Winnipeg. Well, I didn't mind training her and then the hammer dropped. Her fiancé showed up, also joining the business and also left for me to train. He lived at Bob's monster house in Lido Beach with Paul on the same street. I lived in Long Beach about 5 miles away in a nice rental.

I found out that my salons were doing very well, and Paul's were not. They were taking funds from mine to cover his losses. This got back to me from the 'think' guys looking out for me. I took it to Bob. He had to do something or lose me. We have been out where I misbehaved, and he knew I was one tough, young, motherfucker, afraid of no one. He had watched me drop a monster guy about to kill Paul when he was hassling a guy, who happened to be a pro middle guard. This guy was about to pounce when I stopped him and tried to talk our way out of this with no help from Paul who at 5'6" 185 wanted to take this guy on who was 6'7" over 300. I told the guy Paul was drunk and he would kill him. He just agreed and ordered me to move. I refused, and he said no problem. I warned him, which just fueled the fire. He pushed me, and I used a few Kampo Karate moves if you remember I had studied. The guy dropped. Bob took Paul away laughing. So, Bob is thinking I am ready to go after Paul. Then after a few days, he takes me under his wing. Paul rebels and tries to talk with me. I won't give him a chance. I had built a super sales team. We had collectively the highest closing average it the entire chain.

We had a meeting of the whole chain at the Plaza Hotel in Manhattan. This was very interesting because my salons were beating each area full gross monthly. The Chicago all-star was an egomaniac, named Val. He was the Paul for Bob's ex-partner, and some of the old Winnipeg closers worked for him. It was actually nice to see them. The German lady said it was no surprise to her to hear about me. We had a good chat. She was always down to earth and was unimpressed with Val, but the money was good. There was a lady from Seattle, and later her team was moved to NYC. She was the opposite of the slam-dunk closers. She was soft spoken, and her number one was too. I liked their management style. She had trained Val and watched him go rogue. She had no time for his style. I wanted to join her group later, but there was no way Paul would let go what I had built.

I asked Bob to make a deal. He did come up with an alternative when I eventually forced the issue. Here we are in the huge broad room. I was asked by Bob and Paul to prepare a speech on my closing average and how I was running my clubs. I took two weeks preparing. I am a little nervous and start slowly. Val interrupts me and says, "Get to the point." I go into qualifying questions, and he interrupts me again. This time, "We all do this, give me something new." The lady tells Val he is being rude and some of us want to hear how Errol has a 90% plus closing average. Val says, "Because he doctors the sales sheet that why. And my group is killing you in Seattle." Bob says "True, but Errol is killing you. I think he doubled you last month!" Val says, "It's the market. He has a bigger population to work with." The lady says," Exactly my point. Per capita we beat you."

"Finally, let us say there are three cities and you are second. Maybe if you shut up, you might learn something, but you'd still be second." They all laughed. He said, "Trade me markets and see." It was a bunch of ego dick slinging. I didn't get to finish. We took a break, and I introduced my right fist to Val's solar plexus, sending him to his room crying. When we returned, I informed the group that Val has a stomachache and wished to be excused. Bob instantly knew what I had done.

Then they partied and got drunk. What a waste of time and money. My last year in New York, I started taking weekends off. I had a good staff, and they liked getting all the leads to close. I spent less time in the salons and no time with Paul. Melt and the investment bankers became my focus. On one weekend, I would take the red eye Friday night to Hawaii. There my lady realtor would have a host of properties to view. She listed them from best down. I would see my card group and stay in my condo office.

I would make offers and see where we'd go. On Sunday, I would take the offers that we had a deal on or close back with me to New York. The next week we would firm up what we were buying, and I would fly to Europe with the offers. The bankers there would fund or guarantee the mortgage though the Hawaiian bank. I would come up with ten percent down. The next week I would go back to Hawaii and close the deals and look at new ones.

We would rent them out or renovate them for resale. This went well, but I was always short of cash for the down payment also some required more than ten percent down, and there were renovation costs. I did get a line of credit but used it up quickly. I had to sell some of the marina property to cover.

It was clear that I didn't want to work with Paul and Bob was not going to be able to make a deal. At one time, he had us both over to his house. We all took a long walk on the beach. Bob was between when things got heated. We made no headway. Bob had acquired another Paul named Russell who had a record for charging credit cards without authorization from the cardholder. He had built some spas, nice ones too, but was a poor operator. He could put a deal together and open in up-state New York.

Paul had brought in a super salesperson, Arthur. This fellow was the best closer I have ever seen. He was cool too, a real ladies' man. Like all of us in this business, he had issues. I was to train him, but he knew the deal. Paul pulled him to one of his clubs right away. Arthur lived in my house, rent-free. Paul was to pay but never did. Arthur was so entertaining I didn't care. He partied much harder than he worked. Paul was trying the same ego control bullshit that he pulled on me, but Arthur was just too smart.

I bring him up because he comes in and out of my life until he tried to screw me and ended up screwing himself.

Bob asked me to go upstate New York as soon as Russell quit. He was building two other spas with outside money and was just taking the paycheck from Bob until his other clubs were ready. It was funny, as Arthur left around the same time.

There was a ton of mess Arthur left behind. He would promise anything to close the deal. He would never put it in writing and when the members asked for what they had been promised it was news to the company.

I went upstate and cleaned up a massive mess. Turned the salons profitable in three months. Bob then said he had a deal for me. I could run the four spas in Winnipeg and own them if I would accept the debt. I was loyal to Bob, and he would feel it.

I left the Big Apple bound for Winnipeg.

BACK IN PEG!

I had learned a great deal in New York mostly what not to do in business, but the added bonus of the think tank boys was great. It was a positive experience and molded a great deal of what I would become.

Paul had bitched about me leaving and getting paid for my 25% with several million-dollar spas. Henry was running Winnipeg with the promise of being brought to New York to join the party. With me coming into town he could exit. He, I think, felt cheated for not getting down there earlier. I never knew the inner workings of the dynamics between Henry and Bob. It didn't affect me, so I just kept my head down and worked.

Winnipeg was a mess when I showed up. The staff was negative; the spas were dirty and neglected. Even the equipment was broken or needed maintenance. I didn't find out the core issue for a month. I thought Henry was just not interested in the clubs. The problem was cash flow. Bob was the owner, and his mentor Ray was squeezing him.

There were four clubs throughout the city. I had worked a few shifts at three of them. The largest club was in the most upscale area of Winnipeg. I was disappointed with what I had inherited. The gross revenue for the entire city was less than what we were doing at the Main Street club in the past. Where to start? There was an office down a hallway in the large club. I made that my mission control. I went to Main Street because that was the club I knew well. I made a to-do list and interviewed the staff. They were making a sale every other day. The sales guy that called himself the manager was a beauty. He was the most negative person I had ever encountered in this industry. He was not too happy to meet me. I am sure he saw me as this young punk in his eyes trying to tell him how to run his club. I needed bodies, so started working with him. Every suggestion I made he countered with, "There has been no company support." In checking, he was right, the ad budget was very low. There were no in-house promotions, and they were understaffed. When

I asked what he was doing to change things from within, he set me straight. "He showed up, opened the spa, and made sure the pools work and gave a "GOOD PITCH" to any leads that came in." "What about the guest passes?" I asked, "We give them out, but no one wants to bring a guest." Twice, I had to turn the music on when I dropped by. He was either out having a smoke, getting coffee or in his office drinking coffee. He wore jeans to work. The staff, when tested on his proclivity for laziness, knew nothing.

Oh boy, what did I get myself into? To further complicate things, I had agreed to assume all the liabilities. Ernie B. was the companies' comptroller. I think he worked for the public company as I got into a few phone fights with him over the money; well, bills not being paid. When it got too heated, he would hang up on me. Jim, who was president of the public company would call me back. We had two finance companies handling our paper; one owned by Ray and the other by Bob.

I had a list of repairs for each club. My first order of business was to make them presentable and functional. I had a list of suppliers and maintenance companies and started booking appointments to get scheduled for them. I found out all had not been paid and had no interest in working for us. Then I got the list of liabilities; three hundred thousand dollars plus. Most of these bills were sixty to one hundred and twenty days overdue. The city nut is about forty-four thousand a month including payroll, which I found out, can sometimes be later. I really couldn't blame the people for their poor attitude towards the company. This work environment sucked big time.

One of my personal goals was about to be crossed off. I rented the penthouse of the tallest building in the city. It was fully furnished; a sub-lease for one year. I wanted a penthouse apartment ever since I saw the Think Tanks' places. It is funny how metaphysics works; I got what I envisioned but in Winnipeg. My brother could stay the night, which was very cool. It was very impressive to all that visited. A little ego, well a lot of ego was slipping out. I felt like a big deal, from a couch at Thelma's to a basement apartment, to

Ross's place to my own Penthouse. It also impressed the ladies.

Well, now I understood the lay of the land. I had to get my suppliers back. I went to see them all and got many rejections. I can't say I blamed them. I wouldn't work for no pay either, yet I was doing that now. I could not draw a check. There was just enough for rent and payroll.

Later, I would learn the phrase, "How do you eat an elephant?" "One bite at a time." I started at the easiest club to clean up; the one where I had my office. I scheduled a full staff meeting at another club with a huge lobby; great for meetings. One of the suppliers suggested he work for cash and would set the debt back for payment when we got on our feet. I had shared my story with him. He was young and took over his business from his father. He became my workout partner. He also could fix about anything. I took him up on it. We fixed up two clubs to start. The one I would work in, and the other we worked out at since the spa area was falling apart.

My first month, sales picked up immediately at the club where I was working, but very little movement at the others. I tried to motivate the staff but it was burning me out. I could not figure out how to be in four places at once. I would figure management out for many years to come. That is optimum management. I was functional and did get results, but with not much time.

I placed small ads for staff and worked the floor with my people. We turned the club around. The place was clean, members were having fun, and we started pushing for their results. We called old members back, and our daily traffic grew. Along with that, so did sales and the general attitude in the club. I would have the other staff over to train with us and have some fun. Some of the staff responded, but the sales staff was just too burned out.

I tried a promotion in the city; twenty days for twenty dollars "Try us you'll like us." Guest traffic increased but the closing ratio did not; except in my location. I would go to the other spas and close business but the staff wouldn't.

My friend/supplier informed me that he didn't get his check for the first invoice. I had checked it and sent it to Ernie personally with a note on what I was doing with him and now three other suppliers that took the same deal. They also contacted me.

Sales for the city were up twenty-five thousand, and it was good paper, all file one, as we had received the report. I had words with Ernie, heated words, as he was making me a liar to my suppliers. The clubs were cleaned up; they were doing their job, and we were not paying them. "WHY?" He told me to shut up and listen. Then he explained that the finance company was not fronting the money, they were paying only out of monthly collections. Ray thought Winnipeg would close and he would be stuck with the paper. There was another more sinister reason that would materialize later.

I went to and asked the guy running Bob's finance company if he would buy the paper as it was notes that I could sell. He was excited, but then told me they didn't have the money to front either. He did say he was right here in Winnipeg and could collect the money quicker. I asked him how much he was collecting now, and it was about twenty thousand a month, which he was sending to Vancouver.

I asked Ernie about that, and he informed me Bob owed the company a great deal of money and they were using those funds to pay it down. I said, "I don't owe that debt unless it was part of the Winnipeg debt I inherited." I am sure he wasn't supposed to tell me, but it was not. I wanted and needed that cash. That didn't pay my suppliers, and I could see that my sales improvement was not going to help if I didn't get the contract payouts.

Well, well. I had turned things semi around only to find it was doing no good. I could see why Henry was so happy to leave. Number one, and most paramount in my mind was the suppliers. They had taken me at my word and done the work. I had my own cash just in the high four figures here in the bank, earmarked for some other use but I paid all the bills the next day. I opened a company bank account and placed the cash in that account then wrote and delivered the checks personally to the four guys that were working with me. I then told them to bill me directly. I found out through a lawyer that the Finance company Bob had in Winnipeg was a part of the spa package I acquired. He must not have realized that, or just plain forgot as I would find out later the pressure he was under as things in New York were not going so well; in fact terrible.

I went to the manager of Bob's finance company with the paperwork and informed him I was his boss. He, of course, questioned it and I showed him documents. Next month's money was not going to Vancouver. Then I got an appointment with Ray's finance manager who was also in Winnipeg. They would collect the contracts and promissory notes from the other three clubs and process them. Bob's company was doing only the one club I was working. So, the finance company I was selling the paper to has no money to pay out. Also, that money was going to Bob's debt. What a mess!

I got credit card approval and opened a merchant account with my new bank. The 5% commission sounded a whole lot better than the 30%. I was paying. Then I had to deal with staff. He was a good one. The guy that was running Bob's finance company was a smart guy. Most Winnipegger's are nice Midwest folks, and he was one. He was well educated right at the University of Manitoba. I was going to take all my account's payables away from Vancouver, so I could get some control of my sales income. I hired him and paid him a month in advance. Since he hadn't gotten paid in two months, he took the job. He was an accountant and knew finance. He told me about Ray's guy, and when I got to the nicely appointed office, he made me wait twenty minutes while he made personal phone calls to girlfriends as he left his door opened and used a speakerphone. He was a good-looking guy and was sure I overheard his banter. He was quite taken with himself as he showed me in.

He made it a point to let me know that my request to read the paper should go through channels, but since we were here, he would accommodate me as it was within his power. This guy should have been dating himself. I asked for a sampling of the last three month's paper. I learned the term "reading the paper" from the file two issues I had in New York. It simply means we are going to review the credit sheet and see why it was placed wherever it went. He also was, and did provide me with all the total package of paper his company was holding for my spas.

We chatted, and I asked if he knew the other finance manager. "Yes" was his reply. I wanted another experienced set of eyes on the paper; someone versed in buying those things. He showed up and I asked if he could join us. Another cup of coffee was brought, and this far superior man than we, walked us through about forty notes. It was very clear that he had been instructed to file two all paper, since we had no file one, for over a year. We asked to see a few years back and he said it was too much work. I told him of my purchase and that there would have to be a full audit of all the paper they held. He wasn't concerned as their accounting was in tack.

My guy asked about one contract. He later told me he just wanted to see the reaction he would get. This one, he said the person had lived in the same house for almost fifty years and the same job with the phone company for thirty with a clean sheet (credit report) so, why file two? Mister Wonderful sat up in his seat and said, "You know the deal. You could fold any month now and were not going to be holding the bag." Then he informed us that it is going to be month to month until he tells us otherwise. "Make an appointment with my girl for the audit." The meeting was over. He dismissed us.

Downstairs we were walking to our cars and I asked, "Could anyone buy those notes?"

He asked me, "What are you thinking?" I asked again and he said, "Yes." "I want that money," I responded.

I got a copy of the promissory notes and asked him to schedule the audit for next week.

I wasn't sure what I was going to do and I had to prepare that night for a meeting with all the staff the next morning. I wanted to get over to Main Street, as there was a problem that needed attention.

I had a pretty good idea what staff was worth keeping by now. Only one sales staff had quit. In Manitoba, if you wanted to let someone go, you had to pay two weeks' severance. I had been running employment ads all month. I would interview three times a week. I had seen some I thought were good people. They were ready to go. I was setting up a schedule for myself. I would spend mornings at one spa and evenings at another usually closing sales. The next day I would rotate to the other spas, so I was in all four every other day. I would rotate the mornings and evenings too. I focused on where the most appointments or traffic was. I had trained up a pretty good team at my home office club. The manager was a good and well-educated guy. He was young, but a bit older than me. He could sell too. Then, at the small club in the basement of a hotel/apartment building, we had the smallest club in the chain. The hotel guests could get a guest pass as part of their stay, (free) and the residents had access as well. This was in exchange for a reduced rent. We built it out with a complete wet spa. It was a well-designed, well-appointed spa. Being small, many members would use the other spas, which was permitted. In fact, your membership was good at all affiliates.

This was my third meeting with the full staff. The last two were less than productive, but the second showed promise as all the clubs were clean and sales were moving in the right direction. There was a little clique formed and led by the Main Street manager. I had proof he was stealing from the twenty dollars for twenty-days fund. One of the floor staff reported it. She was a pretty, young girl and seemed to like me. I checked the deposits, and sure enough, the money was short every day. He wasn't even a good thief, as the new people would sign the guest register and pay their money at the counter. We had a receipt book and he just didn't issue a receipt. He would put his name and we marked 20-20 in the guest book. We had a different color workout card for them that they initialed at each workout to keep track of their visits and to alert sales staff of a potential sale on the floor. I would come in and focus on these people. Our not so smart manager thought if He didn't write the receipt he could pocket the money, not knowing that it was easy to find the record of the person. The bank deposit would not have their name and be short against the guest register. The estimate was about $560.00. His salary was $1200 a month plus commission, which for him was approximately another $1000. He was the lowest producer of our eight sales staff. That was great money then.

The first two times, I waited for everyone to show before beginning the meeting, but today I had six new people I was going to put on a thirty-day training program, so I needed to start. I had my finance man there with four envelopes and our company check book. The door opened, and "team smokers" walked in with their cups of coffee in hand. I greeted them at the door with, "You're late," and got no reply. Then I handed four of them the envelopes and asked them to leave. I had to add for my ego, "You're all fired." "You owe us severance," one said. "It's in the envelope," Mr. Finance said with a bit of pride. I let go of two managers, and two sales staff. Mr. Main Street said, "You can't fire us, we were hired by Vancouver we don't work for you." He had wanted to have to go with me for some time and today I was ready to accommodate him. Instead, I just said, "You are right, you don't work for me………anymore, not now. Get your ass the fuck out of here." I was a little colorful, I admit. Realizing I was serious, they all left without further incident. I turned to the other two and said you are both on thirty-day trial, "If you want to stay, or we can cut you a check right now." They were both girls; one stayed, and one went.

I turned to the meeting and made the same offer, no one accepted. We had a good, positive meeting. When we broke, my manager from home office came back in to give me a heads-up that the Main Street guy was camped out at my car. I told him not to worry and go open his club, and rock the day.

I had a list of phone calls to make and wanted to do floor training with the new staff, so I was going to be two hours before leaving. Sure enough, when I left, he was still in the parking lot. I wish he had shown that kind of determination with his work. He was mad and had his envelope clutched in his hand. He started, "What do you mean I owe you money?" I just smiled. He seemed to want to block my way. "I called Vancouver," he informed me. "Funny, so did I," I bullshitted him. "Look, you didn't cover your tracks very well we have all the proof if you want to go to jail if I ever see you again I will bring charges. I have two years to charge you per the information I received from the police officers I spoke with last week."

I wanted to him to start something, but he was defeated, and I saw no reason to take it further. I got in my car and drove off never hearing from him again. This wouldn't be the last time I would deal with theft. Anytime you have cash, there is an opportunity for people to steal.

Well, it was audit day. My finance guy and I arrived and were placed in the waiting room for a little power control gamesmanship. This guy loved the chance to show his superiority. He made us wait almost an hour. There was a table set up in his office with all the notes and files placed there neatly. We walked in, and his girl showed us the years still active and under collection by them. They had done a good job of preparation. The fact was, the notes were mine, and if they had not paid out, I could request them back at any time. I was going to do so that day.

They had been operating on a file two situation for almost two years just choking the hell out of these locations. I listened to her explain. Then took a box from the floor and proceeded to fill it with the notes. They were small with the credit applications and spa contract attached. We at the spa level didn't have a copy, so these were the originals.

Mr. Wonderful was at his desk making phone calls acting important. We were ready to go before he realized what we were doing. He came out from behind the desk yelling something I don't remember, but he did grab me. In seconds, he was on the floor, and we were gone.

A few hours later Vancouver was calling. First Ernie, and later, Jim, and they were both cool. Jim was on the humorist side, kind of laughing and asked what I was going to do. "Well, Jim, I am not sure but if all that paper is file two, we might as well collect it in Bob's finance company." That seemed to be the right answer, as I would find out those funds paid down Bob's loans to them. To the mother company, it made no difference who paid them the money. The real point was I did assume the liabilities for the city, but I didn't assume Bob's debt. They simply forgot to include it, so I didn't owe it. In fact, for the last three months, all the funds paid out were owed to me.

We spent two days calling and redirecting the payments to our address. We didn't get all the payments. We offered a little discount if they wanted to cash out or use their credit card. This was cheaper than the 30% we were paying. Many of the people were inactive (paying but not attending) and we invited them back. Many came, and we used a different color card for them to make sure they received extra special attention. We did have some hesitance. For those, they could bring their money directly to our offices at the Big spa. The result was instant cash flow. By this time, we were over 60% cash and credit card on membership sales. Our closing percentages were up. We had very little pressure selling, as guests received a two-week pass. We focused on results and had fun again.

When we had the numbers all together, I found that the notes we had were saleable and approached a finance company to buy them. My finance man worked out the details with their staff and legal team, and we factored the paper for half what we were paying. This was a different type of sale; it was full recourse. This meant if the members didn't pay, I would owe the money back to the finance company and have to collect myself. The agreement we were under with our company was non-recourse paper, hence the 30% for their risk.

If we were feeding the new finance company good paper, we would have little charge back, so it was worth the risk. I was moving away from finance as the last option for closing a deal. In less than a month from that move, we were cash positive. Now I could deal with the debt of which there were some pressing issues. The suppliers that worked with me, I offered the most 50% in cash now. The one guy that worked with me got paid out in full. The ones that wanted to forget our name and never do business with us again (and I didn't blame them) I offered a dime on a dollar or nothing. Most just took it and a few threatened lawsuits, but none did. I was now debt free, and the cash was flowing. We were well over a hundred grand a month in sales and growing. Things looked good.

Disaster was closer than I thought. I was stepping on some pretty big toes, and I couldn't see it from my limited view. In addition, my Dad had remarried to a nice,

(I thought), lady with a 14-year old daughter. He was driving a cab for Uncle Chuck again after a failed attempt at a delivery company set up by Chuck. I don't know the real story. I would assume laziness, but Dad said he hurt his back again. Chuck just wouldn't talk about it. He was proud of me, and that felt good although I didn't tell him the full story either. My thinking was he would disapprove of all the risk I was taking.

Vancouver was calling. Ernie was calling almost every day asking, "Where's the money?" They hadn't figured out I was not going to be sending a cent more. Per my lawyer, I had fulfilled my obligations and could now operate independently. I didn't need them to pay my bills; I was doing that myself. I imagine they were using my cash for other things and paying that loan.

I would see my brother often and have the boys to the Main Street spa for a swim and ice cream. I again tried to get him but was denied because of my age and the environment I could provide. Then there was my Dad. He still had to sign off. He was ready to talk since he seemed to be starting over. Chuck's new family accepted my Dad as they had me. They were good family people. Dad started having dinner with Hersh and me. I thought things were looking up. We even talked about Hersh getting out of that home.

Then he came with his plan. By this time the little girl was calling me 'brother,' and I actually liked it. His wife was a nice lady, a bookkeeper and I would later find out my Dad had told them he was a partner with Chuck and half-truth as in the service business. It was true, but he made it seem like it was everything.

Dad came to me with a request for help. They wanted to buy a new house and needed $30,000 down payment. I asked if he had gone to Chuck and got some bullshit answer. I agreed to help and assumed Hersh would be moving in with them. This was so far from the truth. He played me along, and I believed it all. I went to see the house before advancing the funds. With great enthusiasm, they toured me. They had great plans. It was a four-bedroom two and half bath ranch in a nice area. There was a good school in walking distance. I remember the girl, my sister, showing me what would be her room and how she was going to decorate it.

Then I asked the deadly question, "Which room did Hersh pick?" "Oh, he hasn't seen the house yet." My Dad said. His wife could see this was a time for her and daughter to make their exit and they left. Dad said, "Arie we have decided Hersh can't live here. He is sick like your mother. We have a girl in the house we couldn't trust him with her." By the time he had finished, I was shaking and seeing red. "Arthur," I call him by name disassociating him as family. "He is your son!!! You have subjected him to hell, you selfish asshole." Note: Dad had a temper too, and he didn't like my tone. I walked out past the girls, and he walked after me yelling something about respect. I was so angry I just wanted to leave. He caught up with me at the end of the walkway and hit me in the back of the shoulder. I turned and fired hitting him square in the face knocking him to the ground. I jumped on him releasing years of anger.

His wife was on us yelling, "Stop please stop!" I did get up and said, "I am not a kid anymore." I went to my car then turned and said, "You all can go fuck yourselves. You don't deserve a son like Hersh. I am his Dad now," I added.

I got in my car drove around the corner, stopped and cried for some time. I was neither proud nor satisfied by my actions. I just felt empty. I didn't help my chances of helping Hersh, as I maybe could have gotten Dad to release him to me using the loan as a bribe. I to this day hold a great deal of regret for my actions. However, justified I thought I was, my actions were not. In this regard, you know the saying, do the same thing over again and expect a different result and I was an idiot. My Dad got his wife to call me, can you believe that? She wanted that loan. I answered I would think about it and never spoke to her again. Later my Uncle Chuck checked in with me and said my Dad was talking about pressing assault charges against me. My Dad and I never spoke again. Chuck tried to mend the wound, but I had no forgiveness. This is something I would face later in life. I and urge you to forgive everybody for everything; which is now my practice.

The shit wasn't done hitting the fan. Ray who was a pretty big businessman lived in California. The Canadian business was a very small piece of business for him, so he was slower to react to my antics. It was small money to him. He wanted something else; Bob. He was the kind of a man that collected people. This was their way control, control, control.

Jim had called several times from Vancouver to see if he could straighten me out. They wanted to handle the cash. I just said we have things under control. There was a tempest brewing, but I couldn't see it.

We had a banner month over $150,000 with overhead less commission at around $12,000 a club. I was drawing now and sending to Hawaii again, resuming our buying. Deals were a little harder to come by for some reason. Personally, I think my lady realtor just got tired. I was not there to see; it was just my hunch.

I got a call from Bob he was now in Vancouver and said he wanted to see me. I am working over here, busy, no real time for travel. That wasn't going to be a problem; he was coming to Winnipeg

He sure showed up all right, and with an entourage: Jim, the president of the public company, which turns out to be a mining deal, Gail (a man) and Bill, two men that owned and ran spas in the US, and Mr. Ray himself. This is a buffet of spa power all to visit little old me. It is a Thursday and I am busy closing deals. We all agree to meet at a restaurant and bar across from one of my clubs. They tour the clubs and I meet them all at the club I am working.

I join them, and they are way into the sauce. Ray has his bottle of champagne going with Jim joining him the others into the Rum and Vodka. I am a lightweight and a bit tired. We had a good day, $8900, and Bob brags to the other guys, because I'm still his man. When I refuse a drink, Bill gets on my case, so I take one and nurse it. The guys all have their spa stories, and they are into them. I do notice Ray is the man. The only person that is not under his spell is Jim; he wasn't tied to the spa business. He was an insurance man/public company promoter/deal maker. I liked him from back in New York when I first met him, He was a cool guy, easy to talk to, very direct and it seemed he liked me too. There was no business discussed that night. A few of my sales ladies showed up. These guys had invited them when they toured the spas. I was not happy with the arrangement of my staff drinking with all of us. These guys wanted to party, and my girls were that night's prize. They were all at the Westin that had a great lounge act. I excused myself and wanted to leave, but the guys insisted I stay and get to know them.

This was going nowhere. They were more interested in the ladies than me, and who could blame them? We all agreed to meet for lunch the next day. Jim was ready to leave as well, and I joined him on his exit. The ladies had paired up with Gail, Bill, and Ray, but Bob stayed enjoying the banter and drinking. I still didn't know why they were here, but it didn't feel good.

The next morning two of the ladies were late, then other one didn't start until one. The spa I was working that morning was to be opened by one of the late ladies. I opened, and when she came in looking worn out, she seemed to know something I didn't. She had ended up with Bill.

At lunch, Jim took charge and set a deal with us on the table for the public company to sell the spas and Winnipeg would be part of the deal. He did not give details. Then he and Ray left for the airport but not before Ray did a quick rip into me regarding my, as he called it, stealing from his company. I wasn't under Ray's spell and stood up to him saying if he had been doing business correctly I wouldn't have had to, and further, his rates for buying paper sucked, there were much better deals out there. Jim kind of smiles the rest were shocked. Ray was not used to be lectured that way, and on leaving instructed Bob to get control of his Boy!

Gail and Bill were about to excuse themselves; then Bill sat back down with some fatherly advice about his experience. "I have learned a lot, but they had so much more to share with me." Then Gail concurred, and they left me with Bob. "So, are you going to get control of your boy now?" and I smiled. He broke into laughter. He recalled when we first started in New York. How I wore his clothes and cologne. He knew? "How did you know," I asked? He had this great voice with a super pitch. "Well, Errol, the doorman complimented me on having similar taste as Mr. Abramson, and my cologne bottle was almost empty. I switched it out for a new bottle to test you, and sure enough it was half gone when I got back." We both started to laugh. Then I said, "The fucking doorman turned me in!" Then we laughed again. It was a big deep laughter, the kind you really felt down to your soul. He added, "But the cologne did it, oh, and I arranged the jackets too." We just kept going on. I was enjoying it and I could see Bob needed a laugh too.

We just strolled down memory lane for hours. Finally, he stopped and looked at me and said, son, I am really proud of you. My eyes filled with tears. I was his boy and all the lessons good and bad helped develop me in many ways. I did take mirroring to the extreme but hey, I did smell good.

I knew he needed something, but I didn't want to let the moment go. I suggested we go to my apartment and chat. I just needed an hour on the phones with the clubs. We arrived, and I showed Bob to the master bedroom for a nap while I did my stuff.

He awoke a few hours later. I had laid out towels. He showered, and had a snack; then he told me the story. New York was falling; no way to save it. They were out of money and he made a play using Winnipeg as collateral. They filed two papers from the one club were going to cover the loans, but Ray turned off the tap as well. This was dome. No one thought you'd pull this out. Now Ray's team wants Western Canada, including Winnipeg. I didn't have to say it. I knew where he was going. He said it was up to me. If I didn't want to go along with the sale, he would find a way to honor his word to me no matter what it meant to him. I dropped Bob at his hotel.

I needed to think. I was loyal to Bob, but I could give a shit about Ray and his boys. I needed counsel. I was too embarrassed to ask Uncle Chuck. Uncle Blackie was away on vacation. I called Melt and he walked me though what he saw. There still was a way to create a win-win. I called Bob and we met in his room before our meeting. I told Bob I wanted to support him and my loyalty firmly lay with him. He again assured me that there was a deal coming up, and I would be his number one. I had a list of things I wanted to give up Winnipeg, and he said it looked good and they could live with it. There was going to be some additional payouts that I didn't expect to receive. Part of the deal was that I go to Vancouver and train under Bill's people to learn their superior system while Bob put together this new deal.

They let me run the city to the end of the month, and then I would transition to their team. I came out well and won't bore you with the details. I did go to Vancouver and worked for them for just over a month. Their system sucked. It was the same old pressure cooker close with some very talented closers. These guys loved Bill. To them, he was king. He just wasn't my cup of tea. They did have a team of heavy hitters. I met the guy that was going to Winnipeg and offered to go back and help with the transition. They took over the lease of my apartment. He said he had this, and thanked me just the same.

I would later find that he fired 50% of my staff and dropped sales 40% before being removed. I spent time working in the vitamin business.

It would be two years before Bob got his deal together and it was with Ray. I would later find Ray had Bob running some clubs in California. I went over to Hawaii and finally sold the Card business for a shit load of cash. The Vancouver real estate market was growing. There were a lot of government incentives for renovation.

Bob never went back to New York, and that business failed. Both Henry and Paul found their way back to Vancouver. Henry was given the Kingsway Spa, and some brothers were brought in to run a few with Bill's boy handling two as well. It all fell under Bill and Gail.

Paul started a figure salon for ladies. I was staying at the Hotel Vancouver, and we met for lunch. He shared the end of New York. It was a horror story. He was short cash but had some coming and asked for a little loan. I agreed and helped him out. A few years later he did pay me back a discounted amount.

Paul and Arthur had kept in touch and apparently, Arthur had struck a deal with Russell to open a few spas in Connecticut. He called me. I flew out, saw what they had worked them for a few months. I cleaned up Arthur's mess. I turned a very strong month and sat with Russell. He had plans to open six in total. He offered me the same 25% ownership deal I had in New York. I wanted 50%, but because of his partnership arrangement with his money providers, he couldn't slice the pie that big. I didn't like or trust him, so I left.

ALOHA AGAIN!

Since I had a home base in Hawaii, I ended up back there. I had all but given up surfing, and it was nice to get back in the water. My apartment was in town, so trips to the North Shore became infrequent. When there was a big swell, I would be tempted, but things had changed in the water. Locals didn't like the white boys, and even though I grew up with a lot of these guys, they were different in the water. It was crowded, with no respect for the positioning on the wave. Every man for himself and heaven help you if you took off on a local. I just stopped going.

Real estate was getting tighter too. The Japanese were targeting Hawaii again, this time with money instead of bombs. It was starting to seem like everything I wanted to buy at market value; they would pay more and knock my offers on the floor. I was getting chased off the island.

Then came a new idea; "condominium conversions." I had my apartments, and I was going to convert them and sell them off myself, or so I thought. I spoke to my renovations guy; well actually, that is where I got the idea. He had done a few. It sounded good to me, and I was off. I started in my apartment, and we worked out the cost of upgrading the unit and making a show place. Then a one bedroom came vacant, and we would do that place. We set the price, and I offered them to the tenants first, and then for presale as I started not renewing leases. I would go month to month with current tenants and short-term rentals with the rest, which was more profitable.

There was great interest, and I sold out in a year. I didn't do an HOA. I didn't know I had to. One of my buyers a retired executive, a nice guy from the Midwest, a widower helped me. He did it for all of us as I kept my place. He became the president of the association. I later sold my unit and moved to Maui where I got into another beachfront project.

Looking back, it always came down to this: I should have kept what I owned. That apartment project is worth 100 times what I sold for and the marina condos, more.

OPTIONS

I was splitting my time between Vancouver and Hawaii. My vitamin project had what I thought was promise. Plus, real estate in Vancouver was catching fire. I also learned a new word, 'options.' I knew the word; I just figured out a way to use it. I didn't have a real-estate license, and it took like a year or so of school and study to get one. If you had an option, then you had control of that property and could sell the option without a license.

I would get my options mostly by word of mouth someone was going to sell, and I'd find out. This is how I worked. You wanted to sell your house for a set price or market value. I would offer you 1000 dollars for the option to sell your house with no real estate commissions. If I didn't sell within the option time, you would keep the 1000 dollars. If I sell the option, you still get the $1000, pay no commission and get your price. I would make the markup. I would take 90 to 120-day options and the market was moving fast in those days. I never lost an option; sold every one. I became an excellent prospector. I would have my book of testimonials and references of a great job, but more importantly how much I saved them. I ran a small ad in local papers "for sale by owner", "save on commissions," "no realtor calls please," then I would tell about the property. I was always busy. I tried an ad, "property wanted," but just got calls from realtors. Funny they didn't like me much.

This was a good business but I wanted to own and rent like in Hawaii. I had money saved and was earning from the apartment conversions and the condos. Then there were the good old days where the Canadian dollar was above par to the USD. I learned the word 'arbitrages.' I made a profit on the exchange. I started to look for opportunities, and they were out there. I rented a house in North Vancouver on the river with an option to buy. I was doing the vitamin business out of the basement. I was a real estate investor by day, mail order vitamin packer by night. I was living with a nice woman. We are still friends today but never married. She had two great kids, and it was a joy to be part of their lives.

I would offer 10% down and ask for the owner to take back a note. This wasn't Hawaii where that worked all the time. People in Canada didn't want to wait for their money even though I explained that they made more and if I didn't pay they got the property back. This was a different market and different banking as well.

As you could imagine, I ran through my credit line in a heartbeat, but still had an appetite for more, much more. Like Oliver "please Sir, may I have some more," the bankers responded like the play as well. They just said, "No more credit!" I wanted to put up my Hawaii holding as security, so I borrowed like I did there. I ran into some silly rules that they could not take security in another country.

This is another case of learning along the way. There will always be challenges presented; we need to expect them and embrace them. I felt I couldn't grow any further in Hawaii, so I felt Vancouver was the place for me. I had two businesses there but all my equity was back in Hawaii, and I was unable to access it for growth. I wanted to buy more property here and was running out of down payment money, so I started liquidating Hawaii. I should have had a better understanding of the bigger picture as the Hawaii holdings were selling very quickly. This meant the market was moving, but my focus blinded me to those facts.

As soon as the cash arrived, I would place it. This left payments, and at times the rental didn't cover them. This took more cash, and I kept pouring it in. I was making some good buys, so I thought, and this market was brisk too. I did what many of us do, target the lower priced properties. Today I realized that a few prime selections could have turned the same or better profits. This is where looking at the exit strategy is paramount.

I wasn't there yet and bought raw land with no income just holding value for future potential. I started a development with little knowledge, and the trades had their way with me. I am sure there were more mistakes I could have made, but I think I tried to make them all. A new word comes up; taxes. Now I, of course, knew about taxes but in Hawaii the cash flow handled it and I paid little attention. The tax in Canada was, and is, still weird. If you lose money, no problem they call it a capital loss and give you a credit against future profits but if they took all your capital in taxes and you have no money to create those future profits too bad. I got caught up in that.

On the other hand, I was becoming a slumlord. I was buying in a specific area that I knew if rented it would cover payments. There was one little thing I didn't calculate; sometimes they don't pay the rent. The government was on their side too. You couldn't just evict someone they had rights!!!! They could freeload. If you went to court, you would win, and after lawyers' fees and court costs, you end up with a dry judgment and more debt. I did it twice, and it cost me each time without collections.

If they all paid, I got positive cash flow, but it only took a few to negate that profit. I had been to the rentals man, several times, and the tenant always got more time. I resorted to a different tack of throwing them out. Where they would come home and find their stuff out front and the locks changed. I would re-rent immediately. I did get fined a few times, but usually, the people moved on to another sucker landlord.

I have done a great job of building a large multimillion-dollar portfolio. I was property rich and cash poor, and I had payments. The market went soft, and that was a bad thing for my values but a good time to buy. Then vendors that come out will be willing to sell at great pricing. I would offer bottom feeder pricing and bite the hook.

I needed cash, and my vitamin business was what I thought was the answer. There was good margin, and I did something when we started back in 1969. I went private label with "Canadian Sun."

SAVE ME CANADIAN SUN

I had looked at the market when we started and saw most of the brands that we had on the shelves of the health food stores. The label read, "manufactured for" and very little information about "manufactured by." This was an interesting fact. Then at the Pharmacy level, most of the labels they carried said; "manufactured by."

I investigated and found that the description on the label meant that they were a distributor and not a manufacturer. If the label said "manufactured for," they were a distributor. If the label said "manufactured by," they were the manufacturer. I asked the distributors how they operated and most showed me the door. I changed my question to wanting to be assured of their quality, and a few told me who they used. In calling the manufacturer, I got information on packaging and pricing as I suggested I was a new customer.

With this information, I could see what the margins these brands were using. I also assumed the profits the manufacturers made. In those days, manufacturers wouldn't do small runs. They wanted 10,000 bottles per product orders. I couldn't afford that, but it's how the other guys were doing it.

I went to a California health food convention in Anaheim, which is very close to Newport Beach. There, I met two manufacturers and one very sharp distributor. They were my new mentors in this field. I learned enough to build a core line of 8 private label products. I found from all of them that there were packaging houses and distributors of a bulk product and that all three did business with them. The manufacturers would make up bulk products and sell them in packages; then he would sell smaller orders to the third-party distributors.

Al, a distributor was very helpful. His line was called "Golden Sun." For lack of creativity and for speed, I went with "Canadian Sun." My logo design was done at the print shop we still use today.

I found from these men that in those days the two most popular selling vitamins were E-400 IU and C-500 mg. In the beginning, as I was not focused on this business I bought at what I thought a good price from Golden Sun. We distributed by mail order in those days. GS had lots of inventory, and he was a wholesaler and sold to grocery chains and pharmacies in the US. He didn't sell to the health food industry, as there was no volume. I later copied him but for now, just did the E and C on my own label. He would sell small orders to us as we were a cash customer. He didn't know I was private labeling. The "E" I found came from encapsulation companies of which there were two big ones. One of the manufacturers was introduced to me. I made a contract with them and hoped we could fulfill our end. The manufacturer that made the C product for us also had packaging.

Then we advertised those two top products in TV Guide National. It was about $1400 for a full-page ad a week. It was a simple ad with pictures of each bottle, a lead line at the top of the page "Why pay more for your Vitamins." We had below pictures prices with a box to check the sizes 100-250-500-1000 you desired.

Then there was our money back guarantee in a box and the address. We also offered free shipping over 50 dollars or $3.95 for shipping and handling under 50 dollars. You would clip the ad and check the box of the product you wanted. Then mail it to the address below or call our 800 #. Payment was check or credit card. When received, we would pack and include our other products, which were Golden Sun wholesale list with our pricing. Golden Sun could ship to us each week, so we only stocked the regular sellers. It was a simple operation and all cash in advance.

That little basement business would save my ass more times then I wish to share. I would later grow it to a giant in the industry.

My friend Paul, (same guy from the spas) introduced me to a fellow named Rob who was also in real estate. He was a realtor, a big strong Nordic-looking man. He had a project in the Cayman Islands. He had a partner named Dave, and this guy was a beauty. I was interested in the Caymans, as after my tax issue I was looking for some type of relief.

We all had lunch together, and they painted a pretty picture of how great they both were and how strong their development was about a quarter of the way through I realized they were pitching me on buying a lot. Paul had set me up and knowing him, he was in for a finder's fee. They were terrible closers never even asked me to buy just kept talking until the bill came.

Now, this is the funniest part of the whole lunch. The bill is on the table just lying there. The table has gone silent. There is no one moving for that bill. I am in the role of the buyer. They have spent an hour telling me how successful they are, and the bill sits. I wanted to laugh, but just put my credit card on top of the bill with no one stopping me. When the waitress came, and picked up the card, Dave said, "I'll get the next one."

A week later Paul called me and asked what I thought? I said, "How much do you get?" He just said they need a little sales and marketing help. I still had my little loan out to him. He didn't mention it, but he did tell me he closed the salon. I asked him what he knew about these guys? He said he has known Rob for years and just met Dave. Rob had just closed a business and gotten his real estate license. I asked if he knew if either of them had seen the property? He felt Dave for sure, as he says he goes down all the time. He is tight with the owners. I asked for Rob's number and he gave it.

I called Rob and said I was interested in pursuing a purchase. He tried to play a reverse on me that he was so busy that he didn't feel I was interested. It was kind of don't waste my time if you are not buying. I played along and we agreed to meet. I told him to bring the contracts, thought that was a nice touch.

We met, and yes, I paid again. I told him I wanted to see the property. He seemed shocked, as they had a prospectus registered with the BC government. He also was a licensed realtor. I just said, "I want to see the beachfront or another lot on the canal." "Were they different pricing?"

Then I asked about building and what he knew about building. What he knew was very little. Had he ever seen the development? He said he had, and he had gone down once with Dave as they were finishing the prospectus. He said he was scheduled to go down again with Dave very soon and I asked to join them. I reserved a lot with the option to switch. It was written up that way, and the deposit check was written to the developer in Cayman.

OFF TO THE CAYMAN ISLANDS

The flying route we would take to Cayman in those days was Vancouver-Chicago-Miami-Cayman. We all met at the airport. I took first class, and they were in economy. Dave says as they walk by "Send us some drinks" I see them at each stop and Dave has been going to the bar each time. I had a beer with Rob, but Dave hit the sauce. It is a long trip, and we got in after dark. We were staying at the Holiday Inn which I am assured is the spot.

It is hot, humid, and tropical sticky, I am soaked before we get to the hotel. We agree to shower and meet in the lobby. Dave is playing it up, as he is a big man on the island. At dinner, Dave consumes a bottle of wine. We hit the bar after dinner and Dave disappears with a local girl after some serious drinking. Rob is a ladies' man and he hooks up as well. The people were friendly, lively, and enjoyed a good party. I was a lightweight and hit the sack.

I was up early and had a few hours before meeting the men. I put on swimming trunks, and a tee shirt then headed for the beach. We didn't have oceanfront rooms and were on the ground floor facing the pool area which was very nice complete with a swim up bar. The beautiful Royal Palms block the view of the beach from my room. I had to walk through the lobby to the pool and then out to the beach.

It was six-ish, and the sun was up. There were not many people stirring. The lobby staff greeted me as I walked by. The doors to the pool area opened, and the warm moist air hit me. As I made my way to the beach past the pool clearer and the beach boys laying out the lounges for the day sun worshipers, the horizon came into view. It was breathtaking; the most beautiful turquoise blue I have ever seen. Even today with all my travels behind me I have not topped that view. The beach was sugar white soft sand that stretched 3 ½ miles each way, as it is simply named seven-mile beach, with the Holiday Inn in the middle. There was a large beach to cross to the water's edge. Cayman is surrounded by a reef, which protects the shore from the wave, and makes swimming very safe. I turned right and walked past another hotel then much vacant space and a few buildings. It was a lovely walk with the water warm and trickling over my feet. On my return, I met Rob, and we took a dip. He shared his evening story and informed me that she and her sister would be joining us tonight. We sunned ourselves dry at the pool. I stopped at the front desk and inquired about an oceanfront room on the second floor. She informed me that there was a suite available at a higher rate. I took the room and could move in immediately. There was a balcony, and I kept the windows open enjoying the spectacular view.

The Breakfast was buffet style. Rob was at a table, and I joined him. Dave did not come down. They had rented a car, and I was anxious to visit the development. Rob informed me that we were going to meet the developer there that afternoon. He was going to tour me a bit. We headed up to West Bay; there were homes on the beach side but nothing across the road. I would later find it was mostly low-lying land, a nice word for swamp. It seemed he was seeing things for the first time as well. I was asking him how their sales efforts were going as they had been at it for six months and Dave over a year.

He was vague at best. Rob liked control he didn't like to be questioned. When we returned to the hotel, Dave was still not ready. We left for our meeting without him. We drove through Georgetown, which we had come through last night, but there was no lighting. The nicest building was the Bank of Nova Scotia, and the other Canadian banks lined the street. Rob pointed out the developer's offices. We turned into the development a small sign on the side it was a dirt road very uneven and bumpy. There were a few stakes and then the canals. I would give it a 4 out of 10 for appearance and a 2 for mapping as no lot had a number. Rob was trying to figure out on which lot I had placed my deposit. He finally said he would wait for the owner to show us.

We waited an hour, and no owner. Rob was annoyed and verbal about it. It was easy to see he didn't like the owner or the way they conducted business in Cayman. They were a bunch of 'blank, blanks', in his opinion. We loaded up and went back into town to the office he had pointed out earlier. We walked in to find Dave and the owner Jim smoking together. Dave jumps up and introduces Jim like they were old college buddies. Dave was a tall man with a potbelly and a receding hairline. He had a front upper tooth missing that he would stick his cigarettes in when he smoked them. His name was on the prospectus, and he did refer to himself as a partner. I would later find that he was paid a small fee to push the paperwork through. As far as I knew if you were partner and owner you could sell with options the property. He was in no way vested. He and Rob were partners, and as Rob was a realtor he could list and sell at will. They were facing one huge problem; they had sold nothing.

Jim put his cigarette out and stood and shook hands. Rob informed them that we were waiting an hour at the development. This fostered a nice little debate about where the meeting was and who changed it. I just stood there and noticed my contract lying on the table with the check still attached. They had never mailed it, and the check was to come here to Jim's office.

While they were arguing, I reached down picked up my check ripped it up and headed for the door. I turned and asked where I could get a cab back to the hotel. Dave asked what the matter was. I said nothing, I just couldn't find my lot and the canals lots are all reclaimed land. He said, "They are not!" Jim said, "Yes they are!" Rob agreed. I asked if they had the density reports (remember soil inspector) I didn't need them but also was betting they didn't have any. I was right. Then I asked if the lots were even surveyed? Jim said yes so I asked where the stakes were? He said the development is several years old and the stakes have rotted away with the rain and such. This development has not been a priority and with the new market team, all will be brought current.

Jim liked my questions and was trying to answer honestly, or so I thought. He said he would take me back out to the development tomorrow. I thanked him but said they had wasted enough of my time and money. I left, found a cab driver and toured the island. The cabbie was a nice guy. He owned his cab as do most of them. As we toured, he gave me the whole history of Grand Cayman. He stopped and showed me some points of interest. I was having a good time. He knew Jim well and shared a lot. Jim was loved deeply by his people. He was a politician and a strong voice in Cayman.

Jim would turn out to be one of if not the most powerful and influential men in the Caymans. Rob and he didn't get along at all. Rob looked down at Jim like he was something special. Rob never understood these people; he was just interested in what he could get and not create a win-win relationship. I have never understood this strong ego with people that have accomplished nothing in their lives. Rob would play out that way. This was going to be a major event in my life, and I was just positioning to make an income opportunity to pay off some of my debt.

I came back from my touring with the cab driver late. We had stopped at a few local spots for the island's special drink, a "fluffy pussy." I kid you not. This was named sweet but came on like a hammer. We landed in the lounge drunk. Rob was at a table with the two young ladies. I had completely forgotten about my blind date. Rob's lady was beautiful, and her sister, my blind date was a knockout. Rob wanted me to lose the cabbie, but instead I asked my date if she had tasted the island special? She said, "No," so off to the bar we went leaving Rob and his date at the table. The Cabbie knew everyone working there and he yelled out the special. With laughter, the bartender said, "Yeah man, coming right up." I loved the way they spoke. We were all laughing; it seemed the lady instantly liked me. She danced with the cabbie, me, and a few other locals.

Soon, her sister joined us to taste this special but Rob was being a hard case fastened to that table. It took him a half hour before he joined us. He softened somewhat, but wasn't going to drink that pink concoction. He had been with his lady last night so they were comfortable with each other. I was gone, and all over the place having fun with the locals.

There was a beautiful islander lady that approached us. She was a waitress wearing the scanty uniform showing all her womanhood. She walked up to me "Having fun?" "Yes," I said. Wow, she was picking me up in front of everyone. Then she turned to the cabbie and said "Your keys father." He handed them over and turned to me laughing "Put your tongue back in your mouth man, she's my daughter". The evening ended with her taking Daddy home with a sweet good-bye to me. We were in my room enjoying the view, but the balcony was a mosquito nest. They were deadly.

The next day, Jim called and asked to see me. I took a cab to his office. I had not checked in with Rob, and Dave particd at another hotel and didn't come back. Jim was busy with a cigarette going lighting one off the last. He put the phone down and said, "Let's go." We drove out to the development, and he showed me another section that was his development. I found that he was a partner with a Midwest banker. He was the sole owner of this one. He said he would pay Rob and Dave some commission; not to worry he doesn't cheat anyone. This development had homes built. He said his son was in the lounge last night and said I had a good time. The son Jimmy showed up a little later.

Jim and Jimmy were light skin Caymanians. Jimmy had it tough living in his father's shadow. He was a nice guy but had an issue with alcohol. I sure had left him with the impression I was in the same league. Another man showed up, the builder Rex. He was a partner with Jim as well and could start building on any lot I picked right away. Rex was a nice guy but didn't make a move without Jim's approval. Later, I would get him to quote on some building, but never did any business with him.

In the Cayman's if you wanted to have a company you needed 60% Caymanian ownership. This was Jim's legislation to create an opportunity for Caymanians including himself. When we were back at his office, he showed me his wall of companies; all his partners. His cousin was his lawyer and another, his accountant. As a matter of a fact, he was related to half the island.

I shared that I was a marketing man and am looking for opportunity. He suggested buying Dave out and working with Rob on that development. He was very open about the deal he had in place with his partner. I would later meet with the partner. He fancied himself a wheeler-dealer. He was second-generation heavy money that made a small investment with Jim. He also incorporated several companies with Jim. The investment was more of a friendship offering to Jim.

They had done nothing with the development for years. They built the canals and leveled the land; put in the roads. They had in three years, sold two lots. There were three other marketing groups that took a shot with no success. Rob showed up at the office and was none too happy with Jim. He asked to see him privately. They went into the inner office but the walls were paper-thin. Rex was smiling. Rob didn't yell but was very firm with his words.

Rob knew Jim had presented another project as this had been done before, to Dave who got the commission, so didn't care. On the car ride back, Rob expressed his disdain for Jim and was a bit racist. I didn't enjoy that, and told him so. We had dates with the girls that night. I asked if we could talk before we met them. I asked Rob if he would tell me his deal with Dave, and would he be interested in having me buy Dave out if it was a good opportunity. He played it cool and asked what I brought to the table. Why don't you ask Paul if I can sell my answer? He said he already had but didn't. He was just hoping I would buy something. He shared his plan, which was no plan at all. He went off to talk with Dave.

It was a half hour later that Dave knocked on my door. He was smoking so I told him to finish and come back. He put it out in the hall ashtray and entered. Dave wasted no time getting to the point; he came on hard. Fifty grand and 5% of my sales, he said. I asked what I was getting. He laid out the opportunity like it was as easy as picking up gold since he had done all the hard work. He made it seem that this deal was a little small for him. I pointed out that there were no assets he was selling, that the development didn't belong to him, and they didn't even have an exclusive contract with Jim and the Partner.

Later, I would find that a Jamaican named Andrew paid Dave to get the prospectus through, as he didn't want his name exposed. He was doing a favor for Jim. Andrew was a health food guy, very fit and used Canadian Sun Vitamins. He was a very interesting gentleman, and I mean that he was a high-stakes gambler, black tie in Europe. He had the most amazing stories. It was a joy to spend time with him. He would eventually tell Dave to take my offer after he met me. I didn't offer Dave anything that day. The next day he pressed me. I made him and Rob show me their complete deal with Jim. I even read the contract.

I finally told Dave I would give him five thousand dollars CASH today. I had brought ten thousand with me to open a bank account. He laughed at me and said no way. I just told him I had other business and didn't need this, so this is my only offer.

I told Rob I would buy two lots at the net price and upgrade his return trip to first class. He agreed as it would look good to Jim. We wrote it up, and I was introduced to the lawyer on the island that Rob and Dave had used. I got 25% off their commission. The lots were 8900 less the 25% with 10% the balance over ten years. They didn't even have a way to accept the payments. There was no business plan in place at all. What I saw was something very salable. The most expensive property was the waterfront as it wasn't beached. There was a hotel lot for $100,000, but it was just on the plans. The water system was catchment and the waste septic. There was electricity, but with ugly poles. It could be put underground, but they just did it the other way. Rex had six housing plans.

On the fourth floor of the Bank of Nova Scotia building was a law firm. Rob took me up and made the introduction to Haydn. This would create a friendship that lasted throughout my career. Haydn and his family have become close personal friends and golf buddies. They visited my Palm Springs home several times. Again, Rob and he didn't make a connection. I liked Haydn instantly and he was extremely helpful in my career development in the Caymans.

I bought the two lots and flew back to Vancouver with Rob. He shared his life story with me. When we were back, he was waiting to see what would happen with Dave and I. I had offices in South Vancouver and an apartment in North Vancouver in a complex I owned. I was still short on cash and didn't share my other businesses with Rob. I didn't call Dave, and as I said Rob told me to meet Andrew, which I did. About a week after I had been back Dave called with his power approach. "You ready to get serious?" he asked. "Nope, I am busy with my other stuff now and you're asking too much for what you have." Rob had not told him of my purchase, and I found that odd. I was about to say goodbye when he said the $5,000 would work. I hesitated, and he added but that is only good for this week;

it was Thursday. I asked him if he had paperwork. He said that would be my expense. Rob used a lawyer, Roger. He was a stocky man, very confident, quick with his advice, and you believed him to be right. He was hard line about what he knew about the law. At his office, I believe articling was another Jim. This was a GQ ad he was a very good-looking man. We would chat while I would be waiting for Roger to arrive. I had Jim do something for me. All I remember was the bill was for one-hundred dollars. I was his first client. He is still my counsel today and I class him as one of my best friends. Funny, I wanted him to do the Caymans with me and he almost did. He built a wildly successful law practice and now specializes in M&A. His counsel through the years has been invaluable only to be topped by his deep friendship.

I was blessed to have found both Haydn and Jim in the same year and more blessed to call them my friends today. I dearly love them both.

Dave made the deal for $5,000, and the legal was I think, under a thousand. Rob was happy too. He lived up on a hill in West Vancouver on a large acreage that I wish I owned. There was an old house there that he rented. It was an adventure getting to his place as it was off road. There was a dirt road that would wind through the trees until you reached flat land to park. He had a dog, a huge German shepherd, and man that dog was mean. Rob had to be with me before I got out of the car. Then for some reason, he took a liking to me. I called him puppy, and when Rob traveled, I would come up and feed him so he wouldn't have to go to a kennel. Truth known I liked the dog more!!

Once I had signed the transfer with Dave I was ready to go.

OMEGA MARKET LTD

Rob and I formed a company incorporated by Jim. I think it might have been Roger. I was beaming with ideas and wanted to try some presentations out. Rob was a little more concretive; he liked to think things out. I had four friends lined up for a presentation. I wanted to practice and get opinions, see what people would think. The cheapest lot was $8900 with 10% down and the balance over ten years at 10% interest. Our end was 25%, and we paid our own expenses.

I wanted an office downtown, and Rob objected. It was twofold. One, he didn't like coming into Downtown. I do admit we have a large three-lane bridge that gets heavy traffic. I also lived on the North Shore and came in early to beat the traffic and left late missing it again. Second, he didn't want to pay half the rent. Furthermore, he had no money for advertising. In fact, he was broke. I said we needed an office if people were going to take us seriously. We were selling something thousands of miles away trust was going to be an issue. Since Rob was a realtor and we had a prospectus, we went to the larger real estate firms to list our lots. They were useless, and it was a bust.

I fronted the money with the agreement I would take his half out of his commissions. If he would just make a sale, that would have worked. There was good old TV guide. It was working for the vitamin business, why not for us? We could buy regionally and for us that meant British Columbia and Alberta. This was about $800 a week for a full-page ad. Rob designed the ad and I have to laugh, our lead was buy a piece of paradise and never pay property tax again. We had a picture of a girl in a bikini and Rob said sex sells, so he added nipples coming through the top. It looked so hokey; I pulled it after two weeks.

The ad started to pull leads. I started a routine of getting up early, going across the bridge to the YMCA, meeting Paul and then Arthur who had moved to Vancouver for workouts and then we'd have a court booked for racquetball. I would then shower and have a nap. At Nine AM, I would go to the office. We had rented one of those executive offices, as I wanted a voice to answer the phone. I would get our messages, get to work on defining our presentation, and develop a brochure. Jim had material in Cayman, but it was old and outdated. We dressed up the office with Cayman pictures and an enlarged site map of the development.

The more I could get out to see people, the more I could define the presentation. We didn't have anything to create a reason to buy now. I had a few ideas, and I wanted Jim to help with the advertising and promotional information. We scheduled a trip back down for when we have four sales totaling about $35,000 USD. I opened a bank account in the company's name with both CAN and USD accounts. In Cayman, there was no way to register a sale other than the public record in the post office. This required someone in Cayman to make a copy of the contract we made into one page and the second page was the site map identifying the lot that was purchased. I was using Haydn, then Jim insisted on his cousin the semi-lawyer (he had no formal degree), but in Cayman, you could do that. This was the big joke between Haydn and me along with all the other real lawyers in Cayman. There was a one-time stamp duty due when title passed off 8%. That was the only form of tax. There was no property tax. There were a few small charges that brought income to the government, but the tourist tax was their greatest source of income along with import duties. They had a small banking transaction fee, so the bank would collect about a nickel. The Cayman dollar was set 25% higher than the USD. We learned a lot of this as we went because Jim wasn't very helpful. By the time we were ready to leave for Cayman, we had ten sales of over $100,000. I was taking 20% down and Rob made one with 10% so we had some operating cash. We made up payment cards, one for the clients and one for us. We would take 12 post-dated checks from each client. We would collect our 25% percent then started sending the money to Jim. His partner didn't like that. He didn't like us at all, even though we were creating more movement than they had ever had. He felt our deal was too rich. He was going to shit when I wanted another 10%, for advertising and sales materials.

Rob had gotten used to first class, and he played the big developer well. These were the days of the beautiful single stewardess. Rob had dates for us in Miami, so we overnighted and flew into Cayman in the morning. In all my years of doing business with Jim, he never came to the airport. This time he sent Jimmy. We checked and were dropped at Jim's office. Jimmy wasn't coming in he didn't like the partner either.

We walked into a shit storm. The partner starts in about "realtor's work for 7%," and that Rob and I are overpaid. Jim was sitting smoking. Rob said, "Well, you could get them to sell for you." What a start; we hadn't even sat down yet. Jim said, "We tried that, but it didn't work."
I said, "We have ten new sales if anyone is interested. We have a contract so why don't you sit down and shut the fuck up?" That went over well, lol. I got up and went to the site map in the office and put pins in the sold lots. I turned to Jim and the partner and said, "You can put your pins in now."

"Jim do you have another development we can work on without this guy? I can switch these buyers," I asked. "They are sold on Cayman, not the development." Jim is a politician, so this was easy for him. He said to his partner, "If you want to fire them we can, but we could be another three years without sales, or you can take over the marketing." He went over to the fridge and popped open a beer and sat down. Now Rob said, "I'm a bit turned off, I'm not sure I want to be here anymore." This was romper room a bunch of children.

"I think we can sell out in 10 months or less and we have a plan," I say. That got everyone's attention. What they didn't know was Rob and I were prepared. We worked most of the flight and reviewed on the flight to Miami. I did have a presen tation. I gave it in detail and when I was finished they were impressed.

We hit them with a choice close. They pay for the ads and sales material up front and we work on 25%, which we broke down costs 10% sales commissions 5% override to sales manager, and 10% for overhead, and our profit. The other option was, we pay all the expenses and take it out of the payments up to 35%. They win on the 10% interest.

We got up like we rehearsed and Rob said, "Let us leave you to talk about it," and we left without a word. Jim caught up when we were downstairs and shook both our hands. "That was good, that was really good, and I think you got him like he was on our side," he said. He was speaking at a town meeting that night and invited us. Rob declined, but I wanted to go, to Jim's delight. He said Jimmy would pick me up. Rob thought I was overdoing it but truth was I wanted to go.

Jim put Jimmy and me to work. He asked me to follow Jimmy and sit in the front. He walked in after us like we were his bodyguards. Jimmy took it very serious with chest out marching like a solider. When Jim was introduced, the place erupted with a standing ovation. He spoke like a preacher about a bill that was up for public vote. They mobbed him in the end and again I was called on to help as a bodyguard. We went for a drink at a small local bar. Jim wanted my feedback. What could I say? He was great; he lit them up. It was his bill, I later learned. Attending this gathering did more to cement our relationship than all the sales I would make him in the years to come.

They took two deals, and we sold out In 7 months and moved into Jim's development. We had a sales crew and needed inventory. One of Rob's old buddies was a land sales manager and showed use some techniques that worked. We had a machine, and Jim had the ability to fill the hopper. Rob and Jim had a falling out. They were never totally on good terms. Rob treated Jim just disrespectfully at the time. He treated Jim like he was dumb, and he was anything but that. Jim had almost 8000 partnerships where he was the majority owner. He charged them different fees too. It was almost humorous, except for how much money he was making. Rob formed an alliance with another Caymanian, Michael who also was a realtor. A nice enough man but not bright; but Rob could control him, and he liked that.

We did have one problem with our marketing plan. We offered our clients a choice of flying down to Cayman to see their lot choice or taking the cost of the trip off the price. It was about 50/50, and we would send a sales staff every two weeks with the clients. If you didn't like the lot, you could switch or cancel. Your money was sitting in our lawyer's trust account, and your contract had the paragraph: *if you would choose to cancel we would keep the cost of the trip and you would be refunded the balance*. It was fair and worked with the exception that other realtors would try and steal our clients by selling them their properties. We would lose at least one a trip. We finally put our own guy on the island with a big Lincoln Town car we imported. I had bought ten condos, and we have our clients stay in them so they wouldn't get ripped off.

I must share this story, as it speaks to the exact opposite to what I am teaching. We sent our client down two times a month for four days. They would leave Friday and be back Monday afternoon. There were six real estate companies on the island, with only two having offices. Jim was by far the strongest, and the next one was a young, aggressive Caymanian that did make sales. In addition, there were a lot of developers selling properties including a retired Canadian. This is a humorous sub story. You must understand, this is a small island and everybody knows each other. Before we had a man on the island, the others would be contacted by someone; we thought a guy in customs, and then they would flock to arrival with signs: Real Estate for Sale. "Hi, Canadians we are here to help you." Some of our guests thought they were our greeting party and left with them. Some of them bought a property from them. We would find out in many ways. We had the Holiday Inn van with Jimmy for greeting if he wasn't too drunk. When there was a no show on the list, we'd get a call up in Vancouver. Most of our guests would be deposited sometime later at the Holiday Inn. Those who bought were moved to another hotel and they would want to cancel. Both groups of people would identify who was doing this sneaky deed. Some we would get them back, some not. It became a game, and Jim knew who was doing it but did little to help as they were Caymanians and he felt we were doing so well that a few of the other guys wouldn't hurt. You can imagine how we felt! Even with our man coming with the clients, we still lost some. One time our own guy left with the wrong group and didn't know it for hours. Okay, he wasn't our brightest guy.

This went on, even when we put Ken on the island. Rob and I split the salary as he also acted as manager of my apartments and received a point on completion of each sale. He had the nicest car on the island; Ken liked bling. Now, these snakes employed a new strategy. They would follow Ken's car and wait for an opportunity to get our client alone. Ken knew who they were and it was like shooing flies away. So, we came up with a new tack. We pointed them out and toured their properties, and that stopped it cold. Ken, by the way, was the manager of the Winnipeg Main Street spa. He was a great closer, and this business was perfect for him

I asked Jim if we could buy some of them out and just use the inventory, but he had a whole host of reasons not to, all of them political. He wanted to be the powerhouse, just not flaunt it. This was a good lesson learned. Then there was the Canadian from upper BC. They were less than friends. Jim had, as usual formed a partnership with him when he first arrived several years ago. I never got the details, but it was a bitter ending. There was a point that the Canadian approached us to list his lots. Jim had no time for that and pulled rank. It was clear, he or Jim. We took Jim.

Michael was a harmless old fox that had his agenda. Rob liked the control that he had with Michael. I got along just fine with him. Jim even liked the relationship, in fact, he suggests Rob create an alliance with Michael free of me. It was his political way of getting rid of Rob. They were bumping heads more often.

We had taken office space in Vancouver on the second floor of a real estate office. We had three-quarters of the space. In the front of the space was the owner's private office. He was one of the top realtors in the city. We built out and ran evening presentations somewhat like the old insurance company style; get the new recruit to bring their friend and get 50% of the commission if our closer sold and 100% if they sold. We had things in gear. We tried Rob at the front of the room, but he was so full of "I" this, and "me" that; his ego was too big, and we had to drop him. We had it down flat with a 30-minute story; the Caymans, then property movement history, and the last part, our offer. We would have the people reserve the lot or lots they wanted to discuss. This was not for sale just a reserve so someone else would not pick it. This was a great trial close, as if you gave it up, there could be someone waiting for it.

If you didn't want to pick, we sent you home with more information and would follow up. We would then break up into small offices to close. I the presentation had told about the trip and how it worked. We even had a legal form from Roger spelling out how things worked. If you picked a lot, the rest was just about affordability. We had choices, and if you picked, you bought. Last, you would either book your trip or close that night. Either way, the money went into trust with Roger, and would not be released until we registered it in Cayman. This had now become Ken's job to oversee.

Rob was an executive now. He would show up, if at all around 11 am, maybe stay for lunch and leave to miss the traffic at 3 pm. One of the realtors that work for the company below saw the action and joined us. He was a good guy. He had a connection with a car dealer with Ralph, where he had worked before getting licensed. Ralph was a real mover and shaker. He would bring in cars; only Lincolns and Cadillacs from Montreal and sell them in BC. He and Al taught me how to curb cars for him. It is just selling for the wholesaler buy as a consumer. My first sale was to Rob. He bought a white T-bird.

My lawyer friend Jim looked at a Corvette with the monster engine. We took it for a test drive. Ralph had put a price on it (wholesale) because Jim was my friend and no commission. Jim made a ridiculous offer and was turned down. We laugh even today that he should have bought it.

Jim was responsible for my buying upscale cars, and I have, but they mean nothing to me.

Ralph and Al had taught me well, and soon I was driving another car once or twice a month. It was a little cash cow. Rob wanted to renovate his rental. I didn't understand or know the relationship he had with the owner. I suggested he buy the place and the land. I thought he should buy all he could of the empty land in the area. This was prime, maybe not now but in the years to come. Now it is some of the nicest real estate in Canada. He didn't move on any of it. I moved to south, to Richmond and did well, but West Vancouver mountainside would have been the big prize. I did flip a few properties there but also wished I had kept them.

I had also learned a great deal about tax havens and created a nice lucrative consulting business. My relationship with Jim on the island was growing. They had a situation that was created by the trust companies. Many of the holders of offshore trusts had a portion of the money placed in local real estate. The realtors put together packages and presented them to the trust managers, who were buying everything. This created a windfall for many of the local realtors. It was a bonanza for anyone selling property, including Jim who of course, led the way. That is how he got the partner for our first project. Three or four years later, the trust managers came back to the realtors and wanted to realize some profits. They instructed them to sell and got the reply to whom? The trust guys were the only ones buying. This left a glut of unsold listings of which Jim had many. Now Jim was a partner in Cayman Air Line, but he hated to fly. I only got him to Miami once, and we had him drunk ever before boarding. This was just an hour flight.

He showed me his listing file, which was half the island. He asked what I could do with this since we had been so successful with the now three developments. He made it clear that Rob would not be a part of this as he didn't think the offshore owners would like him. He wanted to set up a separate company, which was his standard procedure. I could understand where he was coming from, but Rob was my partner, and I told Jim I had to speak to him. Jim liked my answer. It was if I had passed a test. Rob wasn't interested in anything further with Jim, and he had a plan. We would keep the marketing company as partners and break off; Rob with Michael and me with Jim. We then could market each other's listings. Rob had a few sales lined up on some of Michael's family property and this way he didn't have to split the commissions with me. He didn't tell me about them, I learned from Ken who was going to work with Rob. This wasn't by choice, but Rob needed someone to do the work. Michael was in a better position to get Ken immigration paperwork, and in fact did.

We were running short on inventory, and Rob had the time, plus he was a realtor, so he was going to keep the inventory rolling. In fact, he and Michael had an 84-acre property they were working on. Rob and I would purchase it, at an inflated price that he and Michael would split as if I didn't know it. Plus, Jim knew every square inch of Cayman, and the going prices. We were paying double the going price for that plot. The thing was it was $400 USD an acre. The deals Jim and I had going were massive, so I felt I could pay and just keep the peace.

Jim was very smart; he didn't want any Caymanian to sell their beachfront property. He wanted them if they needed money, to lease it. This was way ahead of its time. His goal was to make them all rich when the values skyrocketed, and he was right, they did. Some listed most didn't.

When a Caymanian wanted to sell their land, it was because they wanted to buy something. If they had no need for the money, they would not sell. I did deals with them for a speed boat and car, six goats and ten thousand in cash. The deals were written up just that way.

We were making more on the 10% interest, so we would rather the buyer make a low down- payment and finance the balance. Jim liked the finance too. We started some building projects, and they were easy to sell. Jim had a ton of property that he had sold to the trusts, and others he had sold to partners. We were going through it piece by piece and picking the ones we could make money. Then we would buy back some for future use.

In short, I was dialed in. Jim was as connected as you could get. If we needed something, he could arrange it. I was his man; I could travel and represent him at a level he felt comfortable with. We tried to include Jimmy, but that was just a disaster.

Rob was getting the 84-acres ready for sale. He hired an architect. I met him and even took a listing and sold a house for him. He drew up a 1-acre lot development and Rob put together the marketing material. We needed inventory badly. The 84 acres was just a month and a half's inventory. We had a machine going. We looked at two other developments; one in Colorado and another in Salmon Arm BC. We made a deal to sell the BC, but it wasn't the same. I oversaw that deal, and Rob was running the 84-acres. He brought it to market, and the pricing was much better than Jim's lots, which were quarter acre for $9900. Rob's was priced at

$14,500 for an acre. We sold out quickly, and Rob was back looking for more. Jim had more, but that didn't sit well with Rob or his partner, Michael. Then we found that this land is agriculture, so they redo the plans to 4-acre hobby farms. One small problem; they are all sold as one-acre lots. Rob and Roger came up with a tenant in common plan so there would be four owners each with a 1-acre holding. We got all the people re-signed for that. I was busy with the Salmon Arms project, and then we got rejected in Colorado.

During this time, I have the business with Jim going, the trust consulting, my Vancouver real estate, the vitamin business, and the marketing company with Rob. I was busy. Rob didn't file a prospectus for the 84-acres. We could sell it with him and the sales staff, but I could not. The real estate board came down on us. We were under investigation. They asked us to stop our advertising and not to sell until they were done.

We went to Roger and he met with them to get the lay of the land. He didn't think there was a problem. They were a bit pissed that our staff were not realtors, but if we had the prospectus, they didn't need one. Their major focus was on the 84 acres and the zoning. In Cayman, if you wanted a zoning change you usually got it in a week. It was not like the Vancouver market.

THE RCMP ALWAYS GETS THEIR MAN

Here we are, just pumping out sales and we didn't want to stop. Roger had told us that we didn't have too. It was a request, not an order. So, we didn't stop. The 84 acres was interior property, so we needed to build a road in. The approval took too long, as we needed to get the property owners to give us an easement through their land. This was just a little oversight of Rob and the architect who hired our survey team. It was no problem getting the easements as it opened their property to the main road, increasing the value instantly. Within a year, there we people building on their land. The road cost us $50,000 USD. When you took in all the cost of getting to the land, the plans, and all the other expenses, we could have bought acreage on the main road cheaper, but Michael didn't own that land.

There were a few more little things Rob forgot, and those would eventually bite us in the ass. We operated for another month, with the Real Estate Board visiting several times. Roger had met with the commissionaire twice. These guys were weasels. They dressed in cheap clothes, army haircuts, except the commissionaire; he was always exclusive and dressed for success.

Rob was spending more time in the Caymans. He had a girlfriend down there and was staying in my condo with Ken and his lady. One day I arrived at the office early; our secretary is just making coffee. The weasels show up with more weasels. I ask them if they want coffee and open the boardroom for what I think is a meeting; wrong! One of the fellows I had never seen before with an even shorter haircut introduces himself as Ron from the RCMP and hands me papers. Now we are officially closed. All the staff had to leave, and they start taking the office apart.

I go out to call Roger but he was not in yet. I left a message, and he returns my call an hour later. I had no idea what was happening. I got a message to Rob at the Holiday Inn, but he doesn't respond until the next day. Roger came down, and read the paperwork and said it was bullshit. "When can we go back to work?" I asked. He said he would find out.

This will lead to the worst business discussion of my entire business career. I am about to find out about justice, and that big fish eat little fish, but the government eats all the fish. I entered a fight I could not win. I am loyal to my partner only to have him backstab me like earlier in Hawaii. The difference is, this time I had a choice.

Later we would find there were other things at play like my tax haven consulting. I wasn't popular with the government. I didn't know this because we were following the rules as they were laid out. I stupidly advertised, and that I could have done without.

When Rob returned, we had dinner with Roger, and he briefed us on the investigation. It was all about the 84 acres with no prospectus. What I didn't understand, was that is how they opened the door to come in and stop us. We were a pain in the ass of the real estate board and advertising tax-free. We had been asked to stop, but didn't, and then we were stopped.

The investigation went on for months. The funny thing is, both Rob and I had other channels through the Caymans. Rob worked through Michael and me through Jim. They had closed the marketing company, and there was some bad press. We were still doing business. A few of the sales staff broke off with me. Another group formed their own firm with Ross, selling US property for the group he had worked for before coming to Canada.

Rob made me an offer in front of Roger. He would take the blame for the 84 acres as it was his fault and I work the Salmon Arm project, which was in good standings with the real estate board. Roger had said there was no wrongdoing and he was sure this would end well, but not quickly. He had worked in the prosecutor's office for I think eight years before he went into private practice. He was very confident. I thought about it and said we are partners; I will stand with you. This was a huge mistake. He would have written me out of the picture right then.

We had a preliminary hearing, but Rob hired another lawyer; a very good one.

Before the judge rules if the case will go to trial, Rob's lawyer had a private meeting with the Judge and the prosecutor and struck a deal. They said I was the kingpin, and Rob pled guilty and received a conditional discharge that he keep the peace for six months. He must testify in court as well. This was without notice, a complete blind side. Rob will not take our calls and refers us to his counsel. I finally go up to the house and see Rob but he is reluctant to speak with me. He did wish me luck. Funny thing; he kept the dog very close to him.

Roger told me I had nothing to worry about and he would defend me as he was well trained in this law. This took six years. The interesting thing is there were no complaints from the clients, not one. In fact, all but one continued to make their payments, which Rob and Michael collected.

In the end, we did go to court and Roger had to hire a co-counsel, Brian. This was a nice man. The reason was that Roger might have to testify, as he had been to Cayman reviewed all the laws there and was privy to information germane to the case. Brain never got a handle on the case and didn't like Rogers's tack. In addition, Haydn was brought in to testify and felt he was not used correctly as he was practicing there and knew the interruption of the laws in Cayman. The judge didn't like me. He saw a young punk ripping off people getting rich.

In the end, they claimed that there could only be one house built on a 4-acre lot so only one of the tenants in common could build a house. The laws in Cayman did say that, but they also said each application would be reviewed on its own merit. In the Cayman population of 15,000, 6,000 of those were Jamaicans, which made up the labor force. The building of a house was a big deal. That would put 10 to 15 people to work. There were houses built all around the road we had built. The application was just a formality. Jim told me that. He didn't see the big deal, or he said he would have come up.

The architect Eric, got a free trip up. He said he had told Rob about the one house and thought I was present but was not sure. Rob said when he testified that he was never told. Michael had failed to tell him or didn't know himself. In Cayman, this wasn't an issue, and building permits were rarely turned down. Further, only one of our clients testified that they might want to build. Just before the judge was to render his decision, Roger was suspended from practice. I think he was later disbarred. He wasn't with me in court that day. An articling lawyer, a young girl, accompanied me.

The judge threw the book at me including one-year jail, fines, restitution, probation. I was in shock. The prosecutor Fred, who was outside counsel brought in to try the case came up to me and wished me good luck. He knew I was getting shafted. He also told the judge that I was not a flight risk and should be released until I am to report the sheriff. The judge reluctantly agreed. I remember walking down the street in a daze.

There was a hiring call, as the judge had eroded his sentence. Roger had said he would do the appeal for free but never got through his own mess. Brian came with me to the next hearing. Apparently, the judge's sentence was more than allowed. He simply said he overstepped bounds, but since it was under appeal that court could sort things out.

I will never forget the RCMP's high-fiving each other when the judge read his verdict. This fueled me to succeed more, as I looked at those small-minded people that knew they had a manufactured case. We lost the appeal using a high-powered lawyer suggested by Brian. He read the material interview to Roger who still claimed there was no wrongdoing. He told me this was quite a mess and he was not sure if he could unravel it.

He got the sentence reduced to a $10,000 fine, and one year sentence, or which I did two months and was released on probation. During that time, again only one lady didn't want her property and said she was going to sue. I asked Rob to handle it, but he didn't feel she deserved a refund. I bet he didn't have the money, so I bought the property from her.

After this was all settled, Rob found out that there was a sizable amount of money left in Roger's trust account that had been frozen. It was now due to the company I was left to run by Rob, who resigned the day he made his plea. Half of the $10,000 fine was to the company, which I paid. All those funds were released to me at around a month's sale. Since no one had asked for a refund and the fine were paid, the funds were paid to the company and then to me. After all was said and done, I made a nice profit.

Rob thought he was entitled to his share. He wanted to know how much and when he could have it. I reminded him that he didn't have his dog with him today. That was the last time I saw Rob. He did call Roger to try and find out what the amount was. Roger said he told him, "Fuck off you dirty rat." That sounded like Roger, but actually more like me.

Rob stopped doing business in Cayman shortly after, and he had to surrender his real estate license. Personally, I think it was his ego that couldn't handle people looking at him in Cayman. When Jim found out what he had done, he was no friend of his. Jim had protected me a few times in deals when people wanted to go directly to him and cut me out. He was a stand-up guy with me; like a father. Jimmy and I always got along except for one night when he was drunk, and a few fists flew. He apologized in the morning in front of Jim.

My friendship and business association with Jim remained strong until his death in1988. He was claimed to be a national hero. He was a passionate man that loved his country deeply. I learned many, so many valuable lessons from him. I didn't attend his funeral or the dedication to him in Heroes Square where there is a life-size statue of him. I never had a contract with Jim; we just shook hands.

I can close my eyes and hear him saying, "Errol, I want you to go look at this property, and we'll incorporate a company. Then you go sell it."

I share this story with you not because I am proud of my actions. If I could turn back time, I would have done things differently. Those were the most embarrassing, degrading days of my life.

My point is, we all face adversity in many forms and degrees. This can be the test that defines us, molds us to who we are, and become. We need to embrace it and push our way through. I think that was as close as I was to the breaking point as I have ever been. To this day, I felt we were victims of the bigger guy having his way with us. I would tackle the government one more time before this lesson would truly sink in.

I have known Errol for 40+ years. Even back then he had an obvious, but raw, talent for spotting a business opportunity and what was more impressive, was his knowledge, enthusiasm, ability and commitment to bring an opportunity to fruition. His adventure into the real estate market in Cayman Islands BWI along with local entrepreneur, Jim Bodden, was my introduction to Errol's outstanding but unconventional abilities. Alas, in one aspect of this venture, his youthful enthusiasm was undermined by a less than competent Canadian lawyer, a dishonest partner (that created the problem) and resulted in what was probably the low point in his career. Having structured an investment in Cayman real estate properly and precisely in accordance with local and Canadian advice, he appeared to fall foul of the Canadian authorities. The case brought against him had no merit either in law or in fact. However, a combination of an incompetent defense lawyer, an over-zealous prosecutor and a less than credible prosecution witness resulted in what any unbiased observer would have considered to be a complete miscarriage of justice. To Errol's credit, he was able to turn this reversal of fortune into just a minor setback in his business career, and over the years he prospered spectacularly as a result of his remarkable ability and commitment. As with everything, he brings that same commitment to our shared love of the game of golf. Add to that his philanthropy and caring nature, and you will find his formula for his exceptional success. Being a lawyer, I am very conventional. Errol is unconventional. One of my abiding memories is about driving him to a venue where he was giving a motivational speech in England. I decided to stand at the back of the auditorium and listen. The hall was packed with entrepreneurs, some experienced, some merely hopeful. Errol

came on stage, larger than life and wearing a business suit, golf shirt, and white tennis shoes. The room hushed and from the minute Errol started speaking the room was totally captivated…………Errol may be different – but if he has something to say it is invariably worth listening to! Read this book, enjoy it……………..and learn!

Hadyn Rutter
Lawyer

I AM A FARMER NOW

Two great things happened to me. I learned to play golf, which has become one of my life's most passionate games, and I started building the vitamin company. The vitamin market was wide open. The health food movement was strongest out of California. I enjoyed that area. There was lots of golf and the occasional surfing adventure. I just enjoyed the beach area. There were many suppliers, both manufacturers and distributors to teach me. I would check the shelves in the large health food stores. If I liked a product, I would buy it and then see a manufacturer. Then I'd get costs on putting it into my private label.

I had tried the wholesale route and didn't like the receivables; they were just too hard to collect. We focused on mail orders and opening retail stores where we had cash. We had one location in North Van and opened another on Broadway in Vancouver, then more. I was modeling myself after Radio Shack.

I was listening to an interview with the CEO of Radio Shack. They were a public company and on the move. He said his marketing plan was for small, conveniently located stores with plenty of inventory and massive advertising. That sounded good. I would walk through major retailers in Vancouver to look at their displays and if they carried vitamins in their product mix. I would count the inventory to see which products they stocked the most. I paid attention to how many facing each item (SKU) and what size they were carrying. This gave me tremendous mainstream market insight. I felt the health food stores were not my competition I wanted to compete with the big boys and deliver a better product.

In those days that was easy to do. Today the product mix is close to the same as many of the majors carry a full line of supplements and even specialty items as the manufacturers of health products just couldn't resist those larger volumes.

In the old days, it was like crossing over, if a manufacturer sold their brand into mainstream retail, the health food stores would drop the line in protest. The majors could operate on a leaner margin and the HFS could not. Their marketing was based on unique and higher quality; the consumer still bought on price. Don't get me wrong there were plenty of customers that wanted quality. My position; if I don't compete on price I won't get a chance to show my quality products.

A great example in that day was Vitamin E 400 IU the most popular vitamin. There were several qualities of Vitamin E. There was the synthetic and natural with a grade of the natural. The synthetic was marked dl-alpha were the natural was marked d-alpha or mixed tocopherol. There was a difference in the way the body would use the synthetic and the natural, but if you didn't get a chance to tell customers, they would just buy the synthetic. We took the role of educating our customer. Most people wanted to buy the quality product. We took a lot of criticism from our industry for carrying it and even move for advertising synthetic E. We used that as a leader and advertised it at cost, so our pricing was miles below the mainstream retailers and the health food store wouldn't carry it.

This brought in traffic. Then we had an educational presentation using the latest best seller Health books. Most of the time they were written by health-oriented doctors. We would use the book as third party sale tools; showing customers what the doctors were saying. Usually, we would sell the book as an upsell. We would have regular meeting with staff and train on creating programs for our customers. We developed an educational section in our store full of information sheets for the use of vitamins and reprints of popular articles. We had over 50 pages, and they were free.

The information was an issue with the government. We had a Health Protection Branch (HPB) to protect people from false information and products. This with the information was a form of censorship as we always quoted our sources at the bottom of each sheet. We in Canada had legislation that prevented you from making any health claims on any product. They even had what you could say about many of the vitamins. Their information was so old it was like "Vitamin C prevents scurvy."

HBP was understaffed, and if you saw them in your store it was from a complaint and funny enough, it would usually emanate from someone in our own industry. This was one of the reasons I finally quit our industry's association. This association had very little power and was staffed with people that would run from any confrontation. We also had an industry magazine that was just as gutless. In short, our industry was at best fragmented. It was a free for all with mountains of jealousy. There were a few progressive business people, but the most were just out for themselves. The USA was much more organized, and I would follow what they were doing. I would encourage my managers to visit other stores, check pricing and see displays and then be creative in their own stores.

We finally put a price on the literature, as that made them legal. We designed a vitamin chart that became our most popular piece. We would give it out to all our new customers with a standard presentation that all the staff had to memorize and be tested on regularly.

There were a few things I wanted all our sales staff to do the same. It took time and follow up, but we got it right.

Our philosophy was there are plenty of other places to buy your products; you don't have to buy them from us. It was a privilege to have you stop in our store. There were two things you had to do with every customer. One, you always say hi and goodbye no matter what. Second, you never, never, ever asked, "Can I help you?" It is the kiss of death in retail. If a client says "NO," which they usually do, anything else you, say is now a sales pitch, and they said they don't want to hear from you unless they call on you.

The standard joke with the staff was if they violated either of those, they would be killed and then fired in that order. It did get the point across. There were a few other things we standardized. We had customer loyalty card, years before there were these loyalty programs. Today all retail companies have them. We would keep track of your purchases and not only the amounts, but what you were buying. We would call you each month and let you know what was on sale and if it was something you used to let you know how much you could save.

In later years, I would be at parties, and when I said I owned Canadian Sun, many people would say, "Yeah you guys call me all the time." When asked if they liked it, their answer was always positive. If a customer didn't want the call, we would mark their card. This was a little additional service to show the customer we cared, and it would result in the cash register ringing; creating a strong bottom line. We would also call customers that bought programs to see how they were doing and if they were in compliance. Many times, this little reminder played a major role in the customer's results. This boosted our word of mouth referral business which is the best new customer you could create.

In my consulting practice, I always share that you can never do too much for your client. Find something unique about your product or service to separate you from your competition. We spent time training our staff, and it paid off, as you the customer could have confidence in us. If we didn't have the answer to a question, we would find it. Then at our staff meeting, we would share the information.

Our advertising budget was talked about for a year. We knew we couldn't compete with the major retailers in the print media. Only one paper worked for us. Everything else didn't perform. We went with endorsement radio on two stations. One was talk radio and the other, country western. The three personalities were unique and had demographic directly in the heart of our customer base. I got to know all three very well. They were all super people. The talk guys were cool. They would do my spots live, usually starting with, "Now a word for my friend Errol at Canadian Sun." We would send a script, but they would just say whatever they wanted. We bought one-minute spots, but these men would say what they wanted, for as long as they wanted. It was their show, and they were heavyweights; nobody told them what to do. This was tremendous value, and they would compete saying, "You tell them Webster sent you. Don't say, Burns," which was the other agent. Burns would do the same. People would come into our store and immediately indicate who sent them. These guys were golden. One day I was over at the station before Webster's show. Both he and Burns were smokers. I had just spent time with Webster on a vitamin program for him and his wife. He was ready to try. Burns was a vitamin user; I gave him anything he asked for, and then personally delivered to him. Webster had smoked cigarettes too, so while I was there with him, I made an argument for him to quit. Then I drove back to the office with the radio on that station. I loved monitoring all their shows, and it was easy as they were back to back 8-9-10 am.

He always started his show "Jack Webster here," then he would go to the day topic. He started with, "I just had a visit from my good friend Errol from Canadian Sun. He wants me to stop smoking (you can hear him taking a drag on a cigarette) he continues. Errol made a good case too I will give him that (then another heavy drag and blow out) but, he was unsuccessful. He did bring a host of vitamins for me and the wife to try." He went through the list one by one. He was on for more than five minutes. He ended and said, "His commercial will be on later; just remember to say Webster sent you." Wow. They both would have me on as a guest from time to time when a guest would cancel or for some filler. I was ten minutes away, and the vitamin topic always brought interesting and controversial calls both pro and con. The country western station was very different. The country western listeners are very loyal to their station and their music. Both the other men had loyal fans for sure, but Bob was a master. He was one of the nicest people I have ever worked with. On the radio, he was outstanding. His knowledge of his music was uncanny. He did commercials live. Normally, you pay the station for a spot and then pay the talent separately. Instead, I would personally deliver Bob's check to him. Bob was a vitamin user and asked if he could take fees in trade. On air, he would add his personal comments but seldom go over the minute. He was just as effective as both the others.

We had six stores at that time, and we would draw geographically to the country areas as well. In all this, was a strong lineup and got great exposure and new customers, which we followed, in our weekly reports. We had a good reporting system that I learned from my time in New York and the 'hellos and goodbyes' from the spas. All the training was working. If anything, I was too controlling, and that was my own issues on trust after my two experiences with Hawaii and Rob.

Trust and staff management would be the next major challenges I would be facing. We were expanding when we ran into an opportunity we felt to be a big one. We were introduced to the Hudson Bay Company's license program. This was going to be our focus for the next 15 years.

WELCOME TO THE HUDSON BAY

This seemed to be the opportunity that could launch us nationally. We were introduced to the license manager for British Columbia, Robert. He was an extremely talented individual, and he would move up the corporate ladder with the Bay to the Vice President's desk. He was all that a great executive should be, and I learned a great deal from him. Meetings with him were a joy. He was one of the most organized people I have ever met. He also introduced me to the corporate politics and red tape that came with a large company. He knew the game and showed me how to play.

The Bay had a company from Winnipeg that was their licensee. They wanted to expand the category as they identified the growth potential. Their current licensee was not interested in an expansion program. I knew the company because they were also a custom manufacturer I had talked to about doing some of my products, but their pricing was way out of line.

Robert laid out a game plan and said if we performed we would get all the cherry locations. This sounded unbelievable to me as their locations and credibility were a foundation in Canada. Many of the major malls had a health food store, and this was a category in those days they would not duplicate. There was another chain that had all the best locations. This could put us in all the highest traffic malls in Canada.

We were excited with everything but the high percentage. Robert made us feel like we were joining a team. Looking back, the Bay license would have been better served to have him run the entire national department. We locked horns more than once with the licensing President, Leo. If ever I met an executive who demotivated people is was this guy. He undid all of Rob's great work with us in a heartbeat. Robert finally left the Bay because of this guy. I think Leo knew Rob was better than him and should have his job.

I had tried to hire Robert a few years into or relationship. My company held huge year-end parties with many celebrities and professional athletes from all the major BC sports team. We were either official supplier to the teams or developed personal programs for the players. Our party was a real happening, with a live band, open bar, and a sumptuous buffet.

We would give out our annual awards to outstanding staff. Robert would bring the big brass; all his senior management, and I got to know them as I found out how much red tape you needed to cut to get anything done.

Robert even got called on the carpet for rushing a deal through without proper sign off. We had locations outside the Bay but in the same trading area. The Bays traffic was much higher so as leases came up; we moved inside their store. Many of our stores were open for a year and we brought our customer base with us. We also were much better-trained staff than the Bay. We had a lease coming up across the street from a Bay location. We, with Robert, had planned for a year to move into the Bay. He had done the local political bull, and the manager was on our side and wanted us. Our lease was now at its option, and we had to either give notice or move. The upper executive powers had not signed off. This was typical; I have never seen such a mismanaged group in all my life.

Robert secured the location in the store from the manager who had signed off, and it was crunch time. Our landlord would only settle for three years. We were now month to month. You can't blame him; he needs his rent too. Robert moved us in without the signoff. It was a move that could have gotten him fired, with the exception that our numbers were so strong he was looking like a hero.

We had some of the highest per square foot sales figures and were always at the top of the shopper's reports they conducted. There were some great upsides like we didn't have to do a build out. All we needed was shelving, signage a small cash desk, and they supplied the shelving and a Bay cash register. It was easy to open, and the cost was $150,000 cheaper than opening a freestanding location. There were some downsides. The biggest, was when they held the sales for 45 days. Their paid out had many mistakes, so we had to audit the tapes. Funny enough, the mistakes were always in their favor. Then the percentage was about 5 points higher than our freestanding stores.

Robert would hold a meeting with all the licenses, and I was enthusiastically attending. After about four months not one suggestion was adopted. It never passed the sign off. One was the most bizarre of all. The Bay employees would get a discount from all license departments of 15 %, yet our employees would not get the Bays staff discount. My staff felt slighted. Many of them would not shop at the Bay in protest. Above Robert, license departments were treated as second-class citizens. I could never understand this, as we were a wonderful profit center. After the Bay's square footage cost were covered and a small cost of overhead, we were all profit, plus they held the money for 45 days, which is a profit center of its own.

Another major issue was the Bay would place small licensees in the area that would need staff coverage. We were supposed to drop everything if a Bay customer wanted to cash out. That means, if we are selling a customer, we must stop and play clerk. I witnessed this more than once and finally told my staff to take care of our customer and send the other people to another cash counter. We even made a sign, *register closed*. That sign went over like a lead balloon and was gone in a day. One day, I was in a store designing a program for a lady, but there were two people lined up at the cash desk that had to be taken care of. This bitch Cathy, and she was one, thought the sun rose and set on her. She felt our entire sale was about the Bay. She was Roberts's replacement when he moved up. When Rob left, she worked for Leo, and she came down on us. Her style had changed to a dictator like Leo.

Leo the beauty came to Vancouver to meet me. He wanted me to expand faster as I learned that had the bonus structure was based on growth. Rob invited me to a meeting, and Leo was there. He was a short very heavy man with long curly light hair. He was a smoker, and these were still the smoke anywhere days. Roberts's office was exceptionally small, his desk and two chairs filled the place. You could barely close the door. Robert gets the door closed, and Leo pulls out a pack of cigarettes. I stopped him and asked if he would mind not smoking, or we could take a smoke break. He looked at me opened his pack and lights up, takes a deep drag and exhales blowing the smoke in my direction. He says, "My office my rules." I just got up and left.

Later, Robert apologized and conveyed the offer. It was every store we open in the next year would be at 5% less commission. We had two, but cash flow with the 45 days was choking, as we had to pay two payrolls and suppliers. We were always waiting for that check. We could work the suppliers but had to pay the wages and commissions to our staff. This was the first time we needed a line of credit for this business. The numbers from our freestanding store were much more profitable.

With that in mind, and with this 5% reduction on the table for only the new locations, I got an idea. I was going to risk the relationship with the Bay and make a take it or leave it request. The company from Winnipeg was still in the downtown locations in all the major cities. They were the cherries. We were matching the volumes in smaller stores, but Leo wouldn't sign off on giving us those locations. In fact, he walked through the Victoria store with me once when they were going to relocate us. They did relocate us often, and it would take months to recover. Many times, when a customer would ask a Bay staff where was Canadian Sun, they would reply, "Oh, I think they're gone." We finally called the customer to inform them of a move. Leo said I could move you here if I wanted too and your sales would triple. Like he was waiting for me to say, "Oh, how do we get it?"

Later, it was implied that he had an arrangement with licensees for kickbacks. This was just hearsay but from strong sources. We put our proposal together and presented it to Robert. We were extremely bold. One, we needed the 5% that he had offered on the new for all the stores; so a rollback on the other stores. Second, they wanted to use to open a Calgary and Edmonton store, but again the other company had the cherries, and we were getting the satellite locations; there were 3 in each city. We would open all six, but only if we were awarded the Winnipeg company's locations across Canada. Three, we would be paid two times a month to give us the cash flow to expand.

Robert gave us counsel, and we decided to go straight to Leo with this request. It was typed up, and Jim, our lawyer, looked it over. He warned me of a double edge sword. I wanted to go with it. The very next day we sent our FedEx proposal to Leo. Robert gets an immediate response call from Leo who tells him to convey a message to me, "Tell him to go fuck himself." Robert was laughing and enjoying himself. We respond with, "No problem, we will resign from the Bay as in the contract, with 90 days' notice."

Leo said to Robert that we were bluffing. Robert stuck up for us saying we opened our books to him and showed him everything, which we did. We set a day to do a conference call from our lawyer's boardroom. It was a sunny afternoon when Robert arrived. Jim was in his usual GQ fashion. He had helped me in several of my situations when I didn't know to pick my battles. In those days, I fought them all to bloody knuckles. Jim was right most of the time. We get on the call with Leo and Jim to review and get everyone to agree what is on the table. He was eloquent, articulate, and persuasive. Leo wasn't prepared for Jim. He wanted to yell at me, but I didn't speak (the hardest thing I did). Leo said he didn't think this was of benefit to the Bay, and Robert interjected that the Bay couldn't lose. We are sure to pick up the sales of other companies' locations and we will expand across Canada. The alternative is we leave, and the other company has said they do not wish to expand so we lose all the stores and that revenue and our (their bonuses that year). Leo then goes to the percentage drop and Jim says it is a non-issue in the long run. Leo knows that is true. He declines, and we say we will formally give Robert our notice as it is already drawn up. Leo finally wants to talk to Robert privately. They go off the speaker and we leave the room. A few minutes later Robert puts his thumbs up through the window. We have a deal which leads to our major national expansion with the Bay.

I've known "Big E" since 1980 – and seen everything he touches become a success. Having worked with, and offered counsel to hundreds of companies and senior executives over the years, I feel capable to be judgmental and offer the following with authority.

While Errol can plainly see things many of us cannot in business, it is not this nor luck that delivers his achievements. Rather, it has mostly been good old hard work….. salted with a strategic, defiant, deliberate, dogged, competitive intensity, combined with an amazing ability to mobilize and motivate Football player, heavy weight lifter, biochemist, manufacturer of vitamins, multi-level guru / success, motivational speaker, creator of one of the oldest vitamin brand in Canada, owner of not one, but three hedge funds, bringing unique new stem cell therapy solutions to the world.. sure..,

…but more importantly, he's my friend.

Robert Heggie,
Managing Director HK Retail Concepts
Palm Desert CA

Note: Robert Heggie is one of the most talented business executives I have ever met, and I have met some very high-level people. I am proud to say that he finally joined me in business as the President of our new travel program.

THE HUGE MISTAKES

I wish I could say I made only a few mistakes but I made many. Sometimes I felt like I went through 20 years with a white cane and a red tip. I ran into so many crossroads where I just didn't know what to do, and sometimes I was too embarrassed to ask for help. This is a mistake. There are plenty of people that can direct you. These crossroads are a wonderful opportunity to grow.

Business was growing on my three major fronts. The one thing Canadian Sun gave me was cash flow. The freestanding stores, which we kept opening, produced daily cash and now the Bay two times a month. I had a girl that was my bookkeeper. I liked her, and she had been with me from the start. The multi-location company that we had expanded to was becoming too much for her. She would try to generate the reporting that we needed, and our accountant would also work with her. We needed to automate.

We had Terry, our accountant find us an accountant named Pierce who in the interview spoke about handling a multi-store chain. I assumed Terry had reviewed his CV and checked him out before passing it to me. I liked Pierce and hired him. The bookkeeper would not work for him. She felt it was a demotion and left that day. We got the books in order, and moved forward. Part of the package with Pierce was an option to buy the business as I was going to be acquiring more companies.

Over the years to come, Pierce would exercise his option three times. The third was a charm. Before that, I went crazy acquiring companies. Since the private label and creating our own brand work so well, I wanted to vertically integrate and be totally self-serving.

We were already packaging, so the next step was naturally, manufacturing.

I was thinking about totally supplying my company with all the components from the manufacturing level. I wanted to print my own labels, make my own bottles, caps, and liners, boxes and bags. I made these acquisitions many times paying more, just to get them. Now I was supplying my chain of stores all my own products. This lasted about a year before the red hit the books and it was a blood bath.

I had made a terrible mistake. Yes, I could give my company all the products it needed at the best pricing but had not included the cost of operating for each company. They were all losing money except for the product manufacturing company. This was leaving the burden on Canadian Sun to cover the loss. What an education, this was Ivy league. It was clear what went wrong. I did not run each company as an independent profit center. They would fulfill Canadian Suns needs and then, for the most part, sit idle.

It took a year to fix the self-inflicted wound. I rebuilt each company's sale and sold them except for the packaging and manufacturing companies. Then, I melded the packaging into the manufacturing operation, due to an issue with GST. The result was long term pricing contracts with the companies that bought me out. Most of the sales we made to larger companies in the same industry, except for the printing company. I made a deal with a large printer who bought the state of the art equipment in trade for printing. That worked well. I had negotiated pricing in most cases better than I was supplying myself. The red disappeared. During that year, I had another area of growth. My management style was to out work everyone. I employed the philosophy; speed of the leader, speed of the pack. That works very well when they all work with you daily.

This style was not working. In fact, it was like applying gasoline to the fire with all the red ink on the balance sheet. I was controlling all expenditures. My managers couldn't buy a peanut without a PO number from me. I had become a tyrant. Funny I would get up in the morning, and I didn't even like me. I would say to myself, what an asshole you have become, and I was damn proud of it too. I had another issue I had picked up a very dangerous addiction, GOLF. I started to play with some friends, and with my obsessive-compulsive personality, I had to jump in with both feet. I even started a sports agency to sponsor professional golfers and deduct all the PGA Tour Pro/Ams I was playing.

I would come into the office at six AM; the staff arrived at 8:30. By then I would have most of my manager's requests answered. I had three staff members that handled the files. Then for me by noon, I was on my way to a golf game. I had a crew of upscale professionals, and we played for a little something each day. Our games got out of hand.

You can just imagine how that fit into my tight ass management. I was unavailable most of the day, leaving a giant bottleneck, smack dab in the middle of my desk. If my managers could not find me they would not spend a dime without my consent. They couldn't hire, give raises, order supplies, or fire staff, without my approval. I once chewed out a manager for buying four boxes of paper clips when he we requisitioned to buy two. As I was reaming him out, he said, "Errol they were two for one, I got the other two free." I just said, "Oh, good job and hung up."

I can remember it was a warm sunny day I was on my way to a beautiful golf course for a 1 pm tee time with the boys. I had one of those beam me up Scotty cell phones with the antenna. The phone was ringing with 36 messages on it. My car phone was going off, and my pocket beeper was vibrating. I had the top down and was on Vancouver's Lions Gate three land counter flow bridge in the center lane. I knew it was managers wanting to ruin my game and affect my putting, so I did what any sane golf junkie would do, I THREW THE PHONE OFF THE BRIDGE.

When I arrived at the county club, I pulled my car phone out and stomped on it, did the same to my pager then trashed them both. I shot 74 and won money. The next day, I enrolled in Ken Blanchard's "One Minute Manager" course. I flew to San Diego, and I returned with a new attitude. It is the little changes that make the big difference. Up until then, I was lucky that I paid well or more would have left me. Looking back, I wouldn't have worked for me. Change your Attitude and watch things change around you.

Ken Blanchard gave me a plan. In the new plan, I was to delegate everything, and I mean, everything. I developed a management by objectives. I would meet with my managers once a week and we would set weekly goals. I would travel to the different locations to meet with them face to face at least once a month. We would do the weekly goals on the phone after they would fax them in. In this practice, I learned a great lesson. IF YOU GIVE A PERSON A JOB LET THEM DO IT!!!!!!

Giving my team the freedom to run their own show was the best thing for business, and soon the statements reflected massive business improvement. When we missed an objective, we broke it down and tried to learn, or got creative on how to improve. If they needed training, I would provide it. It was working so well that we then pushed our meetings to once a month. I would take the first week of the month and see them personally. Eventually, stars were born from this group and they took over my duties. I had worked myself out of a job.

I had met through golf some, of the most wonderful people and created lasting friendships. To me, there are none greater then Betty and Justin. I call them Mom and Dad. I played in 25 major Pro Am events a year for ten years with Justin. Our families vacationed together. I guess I was semi-retired.

ONE MORE ROUND WITH THE GOVERNMENT

The HBP decides to ban Amino Acids for no other reason than a noted Ph.D. Dr. Durk Pearson and Sandy Shaw, made some claims that were picked up by the National Enquirer. As I mentioned earlier, the Canadian retailers could not sell these products anymore, but you could go to the US and buy them and bring them back for personal use. You could even mail order them. So, the product themselves were no danger at all. It was about the claims.

The major issue was that our customers that wanted these popular products would go get them. While down in the USA they would buy other products we couldn't sell as well. This was a major hit to many of our industries. There was a major protest. Our Association and the strongest national magazine did nothing. I quit the association over that and stopped carrying the publication in my stores.

There were a few of us that were creative and colorful. We staged some street theater and protests that the media loved, and followed. Since there was no logic to the product being allowed into Canada but we couldn't sell it. We had the media's sympathy, and they would follow our protests. We staged one event at the US/Canadian Border. We first took a shipment of banned products to the commercial entry port with the media filming. It was rejected. Then we went to the public border crossing with a busload of people. First, at the "Peace Ach" right in the center, is the borderline. We all took the product on the US side and then one bottle at a time, we lined up at Canadian Customs and cleared the enter shipment that was earlier rejected. It became a big media splash. We were on all of them. The local MLA's (members of the legislative assembly) and MP's (federal members of parliament) including the minister of health.

The HPB was not equipped to handle it. We shut their office down with phone calls and demonstrations on a weekly basis. We were forced finally to take HPB to court. I learned if you get enough press, the politicians will jump in and pretend they are helping. In the end, they do nothing. Another HPB issue hit us on herbal products. They ban some but let Chinatown and other Chinese herbal companies sell the product taken from our shelves. This was a beauty, as their logic was these products were traditional in China, so they were excluded from the ban. This put a colleague, David almost out of business as these were his highest volume products and sadly Amino Acids were second. He was a tough fighter he took the HPB to court represented himself and beat them on the constitutional issue of reverse discrimination. I sat every day in court with him.

The industry all pledged to back the Amino Acid case financially, but when it came to payment, everyone, including the Association ran for cover.

This was my turning point for this pathetic industry that would cannibalize itself. I just lost interest. My own industry was unappreciative of the efforts and time we spent fighting their battles. The government was just too strong. That was the birth of a new business, The Vitamin Supplement Journal.

THE HEALTH MAGAZINE WITH TEETH

This was a very fun project. I had a sales flyer that I distributed through my chain of stores. In it were articles, and those claims I was not supposed to make. I had called it "The Vitamin Supplement Journal," and it was a legal publication. It was printed on the most economical paper that could hold color. It was 16 pages in size and had one major advertiser, Canadian Sun. We carried a few products that wanted to run ads and supply articles. Then we would bulk mail to our trading areas. We would bill Canadian Sun for the entire cost, so there no profit, but HPB couldn't stop it.

Now it pissed off the major publication when I decided to upgrade my flyer publication to magazine quality. I mean, how hard could it be? I had spoken with the other publisher, and we got heated about his pansy attitude. He kicked me out of his office. I admit that also fueled me in this venture. I needed credibility, so I went to the writers of all the books I carried. These were the who's who of our industry. I cut deals with the most popular best-selling authors. The deal was that I would advertise their books in the magazine and fulfill through my mail order company. I would make a bulk purchase of their books, which I knew I could sell. Then for the people, I really wanted, I would put them on the cover and do a feature article on them. This went over well, and they were happy to be listed on my masthead as my advisory board members. The big prize was Linus Pauling, two-time Nobel Prize winner for chemistry in 1954 and again in 1962 for Peace. He was one of the coolest people I have ever met. In our industry, he was the word on Vitamin C in large doses. We put him on the cover of our first publication.

I outsourced everything but the ad sales staff. I used a little leverage to get my first battery of advertisers by offering them to buy listings in my chain. To date, I only had select products that we didn't have in our line. We had all the brands wanting us to list their products. We offered them ads in turn for orders. Our distribution would be our stores and the health food stores that carried our competitor. We had solid distribution and charged the stores per copy, then suggested they give them out free, and we all did.

I hired a great lady as the editor on a per issue basis. She was super; very knowledgeable on publishing. She was running a small consulting company, and my work rounded out her income. She also worked on layout and would bill for that work too. We did hire a graphic artist to help give each page a look. I wanted a more professional journal look where my competitor was earthy and a little funky, hippy flavor. He went for nature covers that were always tasteful. I had a major advantage. I was a retailer and knew what type of articles would move product off the shelves.

First time out to the retailer they didn't want to carry another magazine, and surely did not want to pay money. About 10% were interested in carrying the publication. There was also jealousy that I would make more money. We change our tack. We did up our magazine and postdated it. We sent one to every health food store in Canada including Quebec (which was a mistake because it was not in

French). An order from the first order would be free. Maximum 100 copies just pay freight .10 a copy, and we wave that if you ordered the max. The Publication was beautiful with Linus on the cover and a two-page article on Vitamin C that would move product. They all took the 100 x 1200 = 120,000 plus 100,000 to my stores. We launched with a 240,000 circulation. Our competitor had 80,000. I lost money Big Time on that issue, but what a splash!

That great closer Arthur was in town, and I offered him a job with the same option I gave Pierce. I wanted one thing; page three that was a message from the publisher. I was going to hit the politicians, and the legislation has hard as I could. The first article was directed at the Minister of Health who came to Vancouver with the headman of the HPB and did a forum. Our industry leaders were invited and got five minutes to address him. We met three times at my office and were well prepared. Nothing came of it.

My editor knew a political cartoonist, and she did up a third of a page cartoon of the

Minister with a giant gavel smashing a health food store and people running across the border to another building saying "Amino Acids for Sale: Canadians Welcome." The caption is from a guy holding an engraved briefcase HPB, "Way to go Jake." We drop shipped 20,000 copies to the Minister's home running out of my stock. They knew me now.

We ended up at a 48-page format with a mix of 55% advertising 45% content. We charged the stores .38 a copy, which covered the print cost and the shipping. Our circulation leveled off at 187,000. This made us the largest health publication in Canada. We maintained a sold-out position in advertising with the strongest masthead of contributors ever assembled.

Arthur had ideas to expand the publication. I showed him if we add pages we change both the print and shipping cost. Further, there was only so much in advertising dollars available in Canada. Our small market couldn't command more from our suppliers. One Canadian company bought the back and inside front cover for every issue. There was a line up waiting for those positions if he would let them go and for more money too.

A publisher is a glorified advertising salesperson; that's what it's all about in those ads. Most of the Amino Acids and all the herbs we got back on the shelves. I was spending more and more time on developments in Cayman. Arthur was playing funny business, try to steal the publication from me. When I caught him red-handed, I explained he had an option to buy, just exercise it. Gee, he really did, and he and my largest advertiser, a big Canadian manufacture, bought me out.

Sad story; Arthur was no businessman, and ran the publication straight into the ground. Then he tried the same move on the owner of that business feeding his money people some bull. He fancied himself a businessman and maybe he became one. I had one more occasion to do business with him and Paul in an insulation company. I built their sales force and then left before they tanked that business. It was too bad, as I saw it coming. It was a good business; they just mismanaged it.

TIME TO EXIT

I was traveling a great deal enjoying life. There were many other deals in which I was involved. Pierce was running Canadian Sun and he wanted to exercise his options again. This time he had a public company that was in the vitamin manufacturing industry. Pierce had been giving them small volume business. They manufactured and packaged. They were big in Shark Cartilage, and it was very popular now. It was his call; I was very removed from the day-to-day business and trusted his numbers. He had moved us to larger warehouse facilities.

His focus was to expand to all 384 Bay locations. I wasn't that excited knowing the cash flow would be tight. He wasn't focusing on mail order, which was cash in advance. We had for years taken a booth at the Pacific Nation Exhibition (PNE). This was an 18-day super high traffic show. We were in the most popular building where you would see all the pitch booths. These people traveled a circuit week after week selling their wares. We would set up a mini store with big signage and great pricing for the show. People came to buy, and we would do $50,000, but more importantly, get new names for our mail order department. The mail order staff would handle most of the hours and store managers would take some shifts. We could meet a lot of customers and build a mailing list. Pierce wanted to drop it. I urged him to keep it going, and he did. The public company made a lowball offer. They improved their offer and, they gave us a letter of intent and agreed on a down payment. They were a penny stock from Alberta. Pierce had done all the diligence and was going to get his piece. He was excited about the deal and wanted to expand in the Bay.

In looking at the figures, I saw he was carrying a few stores in Edmonton that were losing money each and every month. They weren't even covering payroll. I had a meeting with him, and he informed me that the Bay would not let them close those losers. It was because Cathy did not want to lose her bonuses.

Robert was now running his own very successful business and was living in Palm Springs, where I also had a home. He phoned me with an inquiry from a major US Health Food chain. They were the largest and wanted to buy Canadian Sun as they were expanding in Canada. They were also a public company. A second real buyer made all the sense in the world. I told Pierce, and he went white. He was so worried about his deal. I just wanted a backup offer. We put a package together for the new company, and I presented it to the CEO with Robert in Las Vegas. Robert was brokering the deal, and they wanted me to run Canada for them as he had spoken so highly of me.

I wasn't interested in a job but waited to see what they would come up with. This was very interesting as to how this would all unfold. When the new Company received our financial information, I started to have discussions with a Vice President that was assigned to the acquisition. He pointed out those two stores in Edmonton and asked for some sort of an explanation. I said they should be closed and to remove them from the purchase. This is a public company so they needed a sign-off from the Bay. That was understandable, and I had Pierce arrange for a meeting with Cathy.

She was the most abrasive I had ever experienced. She informed me that she was aware of both offers and reminded me that we need the Bay to approve the new purchaser as in the license agreement. I wanted to assure her that we would have a complete information package on the buyer for her diligence and any sale offer would have that as a contingency. She informed me that Pierce had already introduced her to his buyer and she liked their proposal to expand. She also pointed out that she liked working with Pierce and was very much in favor of him remaining.

I brought up the two losers and their no growth for over two years. She informed me in no uncertain terms that the Bay would not accept any closures. If the new company wasn't going to take the company as is with all the Bay stores she didn't think they would give approval. I took the contract to my lawyer and found that they could not reasonably withhold their blessing and could be liable for damages if they did. Of course, that would be open to a court's interpretation. I was trying to be reasonable, but she was hard lining me. The other thing was our lawyers said we had every right to close unsuccessful stores. I asked Robert, and he said it was done all the time. He had been involved with many license buyouts.

Something just wasn't adding up. Why was she so hard line? I had lunch with Pierce, and interestingly enough, he couldn't look me in the eye. He felt the other company wouldn't keep him on and that he felt deceived by me. I suggested we see where this goes and where his buyer is. His buyer would be in the first position, but let's see where the other offer came in. I also said if they didn't keep him we would work something out. He had run the company for many years now, and I was grateful. That seemed to satisfy him.

There was additional information the other company needed, and they presented a list. They wanted to see leases and speak to our accounting firm. They were doing their diligence. I had another meeting with Cathy about those two stores as they were doing so little, we were both losing. She stayed firm and pointed out that Pierce's buy did not want to close any store and then she slipped and named my buyer. I hadn't told her, so where did she acquire the information? It must have come from Pierce. Pierce said she told him there was a larger company that was in talks with the Bay about a large expansion and told him to get an expansion plan of his own to protect our interests. So, he knew about this company before I did and she had named the company.

I phoned Robert, but he could not say anything and asked if he could call me back. He did and said he was under a non-disclosure with that company, as he had brought them to the Bay, but he had permission to share everything. This suddenly took on a new light. Cathy and Pierce seemed to be working together, but why? It would become crystal clear in a few weeks. I took up office in the boardroom as Pierce had my office. In going through the leases, I found there were two sets of leases for our warehouse space. Pierce had moved us here two years ago informing me that we needed extra space and it was just marginally more expensive. I had no issue with that, and he was the signing officer.

One of the leases was between Canadian Sun and Pierce and the other was with Pierce, and a Chinese group, with an option to buy the building at the end of the lease with 50% of the rental applied to the purchase price. Then he charged us a little higher rent that he pocketed and he wrote two checks a month. This was plain dumb, as it was all here with both checks when I went into the payables ledger. I was coming in early, putting the package for sale together. Pierce was running the company, so I didn't want to burden him, plus he had his offer. Pierce was coming in late, but he would stay later too. I didn't pay much attention to that, as he could be starting out his day at a store as I did. I pulled the actual checks and visited Terry, our accountant and Jim, our lawyer.

Canadian Sun had just finished the PNE, and I visited Bev, the mail order manager, to see how it went. She was nervous. I thought something was wrong. She started to cry and said she had to leave. I thought there might have been a death in the family and followed her out. I asked if the kids were okay and she said it was her and she just needed some time.

That weekend she called me at home and asked to see me. She brought over an envelope filled with $5,000 in cash. She started to cry and then showed me a contract with Pierce. She would get a small piece of the new company and some stock. She unloaded an ugly story. The last thing was Piece had already moved into the new company offices, and she had been there several times. In a pool of tears, she said she would resign and please take the money back. She had not spent a dime. She told me Pierce collected the PNE cash every night and brought her a cut the next day. She kept all the sales sheets and handed them over.

I had to meet with Pierce, so I went to the other company's office and found Pierce there. He, of course, said he was there for a meeting with the CEO about the sale. To cover his tracks, he arranged for me to meet this fellow. We talked about the sale and what it could do to his stock. He suggested I buy some now before the sale is confirmed. I just said I assume you're going to match any other offers then. He assured me that wasn't a problem. I told him it might expedite things if he dealt directly with me. We exchanged contact information. I asked Pierce to see me when he got back to our offices.

I wanted to be out of this business, and now I had to step back and clean up this mess. Pierce denied everything until I pulled out the proof. The last thing was the PNE, and he tried to blame Bev. He almost got a punch in the mouth. I suggested he leave and not to think about coming back. I had enough to have him charged, but that could screw up the sale of the company. The real reason was, I just wanted out of this industry. I had offers on the manufacturing from a large multinational that were very tasty. The few other side companies I could sell to the staff.

When I dug into the company, I found so many things Pierce was doing to devalue the company so his friends could take it over at a lower price. It was a mess. The managers were happy I was back and sales jumped. I met with the Bay, and she wanted Pierce reinstated Immediately. I told her that was none of her business and that we would be closing those two loser stores. She warned me against it.

I found that Robert's company had been close to a deal with the Bay but at three percentage points higher. They were going to take the stores I had not. The Bay didn't want them to buy me as they will get the lower number and then demand that for all their locations. I was in a political situation, and there was more. Remember Leo; this was his chance to get even with me. He had the power, and his right arm here was Cathy. It was getting very complicated with Robert's group, and he felt they didn't need the Bays aggravation and suggested I go the other way if it was real.

I met with the CEO again and he was happy to have Pierce with him. If there were no charges, then it was okay. They upped their offer and gave a letter of intent with a promise of a non-refundable deposit. We signed all the paperwork, but before we could close the deal, the Bay terminated our license for cause. There we a few trumped-up charges as we were failing our customer evaluation, locations were opened late; we didn't move all our stock through their loading dock. This is after fifteen years.

We lawyer up first with a corporate guy well recommended, and he shared that Pierce was in the public company field and lost his accounting license and fined $250,000.

I asked Terry about it, and he said yes, he knew but the action taken against Pierce was two years in court. He had been working for us, and we were pleased with his work, plus Terry thought Pierce got a raw deal. He had no idea he could do what he did to us. All the information he was giving Terry looked fine.

I went into severe mode. I leased space close to each Bay location that we were going to be removed from. We had our entire bonus card so we would call our clients. Additionally, we handed flyers out at the Bay saying they were kicking us out and why. They got an injunction against that. The next week the company that was going to buy us made a public announcement that they have secured a Bay license of successful location doing so much a month and will be expanding into all their stores.

Their stock went from pennies to over a dollar; later we found huge blocks sold of corporate stock. They kept these announcements up each week to drive up their stock. They even had one where they had the key management officer that had joined them.

Jim, our lawyer, does not do litigation and sent us to Greg. He and Andrew are strong courtroom lawyers. They agreed to handled our case and made it affordable to keep us toe to toe with a multibillion-dollar company that did everything to intimidate us over the years to follow. These were tough, fearless lawyers that had our back. The Bay hired a large legal firm and spent a ton of money.

We opened our new location and had other freestanding stores for years. We also moved our warehouse with a big fight with the Chinese owner that wanted to deal with Pierce. In the end, we just moved, and they could sue Pierce. The Bay was trying to get our customer list saying it was their property. They were working for their new licensee. Robert was our counsel. He knew the Bay's inner workings and was very helpful. When he showed up on our witness list, the Bay tried to have him removed saying he was a disgruntled former employee.

We also sued the public company, their officers, and Pierce. They did open a few stores and then closed them all within six months. It was always the Bays contention that people shopped with us because we were in the big bad Bay but it was not so. Our customers liked our products, pricing, and service. The new company thought they would just do the same numbers Pierce had promised. He was wrong, and they all closed. The public guys had made their money on the stock play and were not going to sink anything into building up the business.

The result was a settlement after we were set for court and I had signed non-disclosures with the Bay, the Public company, and Pierce.

The Bay never reopened that category again. They lost a multimillion-dollar business that had been with them for 15 years. We had information that Cathy and Leo were part of the stock play, but it never went to court so that information died in the settlement.

I wanted my daughter to take the British Columbia stores. I felt she could make a great income. She is an artist and a fine one at that. That is where her interests lie, and I try to support that.

MLM HERE I COME

While I was running the vitamin company, I received a call from a very respected friend and one of my magazine contributors from California. He had joined an MLM company in water filters. He was very excited and wanted me to join as they were coming to Canada and he told his sponsor that I would dominate the marketplace. I thought water filters were door-to-door sales. Was he crazy? I hung up on him. He called back and said we got disconnected; I said, "No, I hung up are you crazy?" He wanted to have someone talk to me that knew more. They did call, but I refused to take it.

Next month, I was going to California for the big national health food convention. I had a big suite as I entertain clients. My friend introduced me to this team of guys from the company. They are all here to meet my friend's leads and to pitch their company. I don't know how this works. These men are helping my friend build his distributorship, or, as they are called, his "up line." I agreed to have lunch with them because he is relentless. He had three guys with him. They had a pitch book; this was the first time I was shown pages of checks. This blew my mind. Can you imagine going to lunch with your friends and they pull out their earnings? They had no Idea how much that turned me off. Now the kicker was, only one of the checks belonged to one of the guys at the table. The other two didn't have a check to show.

I hammered them on their earnings since they brought it up. They showed me the product and then the crazy marketing plan with steps and qualifications. I didn't understand any of it. They did try a weak ass close, and I didn't answer so they did and lost. The one good thing they did was hook up a filter to my tap in my suite. Later that night they all came back up with a portable handheld travel filter and did a sales demo that shows the unit takes the chlorine out of the water. This was now making sense to me.

My friend kept telling me to buy the $25,000 entry package. Later I found out he would get a $4000 commission. Then, they got me on a call with their biggest player to help close me; it didn't work. I had more objections than they could overcome. That night I used the filter and read the literature. Next morning, I took the units to the kitchen. I asked the chief if we could do an experiment. He was a nice guy and let me. The literature said it would make all products you mix with water taste better. We made coffee, orange juice, and plain ice water. I knew plenty of the people having breakfast from the industry. I asked for their help, and they all agreed that there was a dramatic taste difference.

One of my friends asked if I was going to carry the product and gave me an order for 300 units. I didn't even know the wholesale price so quoted him 179 which I heard was the retail price. I felt I could always give him a discount when I found out costs. I liked the results of the test, five people wanted to buy one, and I have a $50,000 300-unit order. If any of you understand MLM, you can see that I had no idea how it worked. My friend was one of the keynote speakers at the convention, so he was staying at the hotel. I called his room and asked him to come down.

He showed up, and I wanted to get the best price per unit cost to fill my order. He is in the same boat as me. He called one of the guys that were at lunch. It took the guy two hours to arrive. I told him my needs and all he could do was show me the marketing plan. I just wanted their best price. He was so frustrated trying to explain that everyone pays the same price. What, no discounts for volume? We go up to my room and get the big guy on the phone; David and the surfer guy who I liked, and we knew other surfers (from my surfing days), his name was George. They tried to plan explain the marketing. I stopped them and said, "Then this is the best wholesale price there is, no matter what the volume. Ok, this is like Amway?" I then asked for that $102,000 check they were showing and the phone number of the guy who earned it.

I called the guy, and he said he earned it in his second month. He avoided telling me what we earned after that, so I assumed it was less. Then I called Jim my lawyer in Vancouver and said I would be faxing up a check and I wanted him to get our bank to see if it was cashed and to get data on the company. If it would check out, I would give it a shot. Management was running all my other companies and I wanted something new.

It all checked out and the entry investment was secured by inventory so there was little risk if you turn the product. I needed more input and there were meetings up and down the coast. They called them "opportunity and training meetings." I was informed of the up line above my friend Rob. Above him was Michael, then George and David. They all pledged to help me, and Rob did. I stayed an extra week and attended each and every meeting and training.

Rob did know the industry, in fact, he and his wife were in several MLM companies. He smelled money and kept me close. He attended many of the meetings but couldn't understand why I wanted to attend so many. I had a few friends in the area attend with me as well, just to get their opinion. The last day I placed my order and flew back to Vancouver. From the airport, I phoned Paul and wanted to see him. I knew he needed money, so he could join me. Paul had been in a company that he had become a major player in, and it failed, so he wanted to detour me.

I found small ads in the sales section of a major newspaper and called. Sure enough, there were people recruiting for this company. One group was sponsored by David and we would go head to head with them later. I built my team just as the manual said and started running five meetings a day in my office. When we got too big, we ran the evening meeting at a hotel as I had seen in California. I had taped all the meetings and built my presentation from the tapes. I had a clear-cut goal. I wanted to be #1 in Canada.

We achieved that, and more. I became the number two distributor in the world. It was a joy to work with entrepreneurial-minded people. I broke all the first-month distributor records including the largest first-month check ever earn in the company's history. This would turn out to be some of the most rewarding and enjoyable years of my life. Most the distributor base was not made up of business people, in fact, most were far from it. They all were looking for a better way of life.

What was I enjoying the most? I was teaching, yes I was a teacher. There were downsides to the business. You receive a print out of the activity in your down line; that is all the people sponsored below you. I studied these and found that many of the people were inactive. I inquired and received a ton of bullshit excuses but not one good reason. I did a marketing chart for my people showing if you bought the $5,000 in inventory and sold all the product with the rebated and retail income you would make 162% return on your investment. The best part, so I thought was the return could be earned as fast as you sold the units. If it took you a year to make I think 28 sales, what a return you receive for the year on investment. Even two years still better than the bank!

The education in this business was just beginning I met some incredibly talented people and a bunch of egotistical jerks. The two best of the best were Jeff and Jay. Jeff was the #1 distributor in the world and Jay was the president and owner. They were two of the finest leaders you would ever want to know. I became a partner with Jeff in a support material company that we did very well with. I sold it to him before I left. Jay became a golf buddy, and at one time I felt very close and loyal to him and his company.

I also started many distributors out if they didn't have the entry money. I would help them get started and be a partner in their distributorship. Jeff knew this business, and I couldn't have had a finer teacher. He also introduced me to the leaders in other companies, and soon I was accepted in the elite circles. We ran events and trainings for thousands, and we sought after to come to cities and do training. The company would put on two major events a year and schools around the country. Jeff and I became the major drawing cards. Jay would give us the venue before the convention would start, and we would run an opportunity meeting and training. We invited the leaders from across the country to participate. This grew to worldwide as the company expanded. It became a big deal to be invited. I became the host of the convention. Then Jeff would run a focus session Sunday morning before we would leave.

As I look back, I wish I could recapture today those glorious days. Many companies do not stand the test of time, and there were many things that I am not fond of with the model. They are still going strong Jay, the great leader and Jeff the all-star multi-million dollar a year earner. There were a few things that transpired that caused my exit, but that is all in the past. If I have any wishes, it would be that Jeff would be appreciated by the company for all he did, as I truly believe that if he had not, they would not be here today. In all, it was a total commitment of them both that makes that company great. I looked at starting my own and proved my training methods with two other companies with exceptional success, but again the model suggested I could do better elsewhere. I still do like training MLM people as I know exactly what they need to do, to become successful, it ain't easy, but it will pay. Jeff, I believe, has earned over

$100,000,000 in this one company and is still going strong.

Some relationships in life create a positive lasting bond that remains forever. My friendship with Errol is one that I treasure. The years we worked together were punctuated by humor, learning, and inspiration. He was like a big brother - entertaining and fun loving, but supportive in both business and life.

A dynamic speaker, he captivated and inspired people worldwide. He set the pace for entrepreneurial success. A shrewd business mind, with the ability to give expert direction made him a mentor to many. But the thing that impresses me most about Errol is his Big Heart! He has always been a friend I could count on.

Jeff Roberti
Network Marketing Professional
NSA $100,000,000+ earned

OUT OF ADVERSITY, HELLO CHINA!

This is moving right along with my life. I know I haven't shared much of my later personal life, and for good reason, time. I have lived a full and exciting life. I love new things and challenges. There was nothing more challenging as doing business in China.

Some of my greatest victories came from overcoming adversity. I would like to again repeat my personal quote, "If your goals and desires are stronger than the adversity that you will face and you will face adversity, then you will be successful." We all face challenges and hard time in our life what we do during that time defines us and gives us the opportunity to grow.

They were many times I felt there was no way out of this mess, I had usually but not always, created myself. I have found that the creator always gives us a way out. We just need to believe, have faith. Then we must look for a better way. You know what, it is always there.

China, what a place. I found the business and culture fascinating. The people are a bit shy but warm and friendly. I had an injury to my neck, and it wasn't getting better. A naturopath doctor suggested a therapy only done in China. It was expensive, but I was in pain every day and wanted to try. We both went, and although the therapy wasn't effective for my condition, I saw many other possibilities. We struck a deal that would become the most profitable exit of my career to date. I cannot share these events with you at this time, as there are two other components that are still being negotiated for sale. In addition, there are a ton of non-disclosures on the actual sale.

I will say, I have never seen a business grow at the rate this business did. It was simply amazing. These were small changes in the marketing, promotion, product development, and the value clients received.

China is an academic society. Education means everything there. The discipline and competitiveness is more apparent when they immigrate out of China. Wherever they land they raise the academic bar big time. I was and am witness to this in Vancouver where we have had a massive number of Chinese Immigrants. They are hardworking, and have also set a new social standard. I was involved with golf in China, but at a level, I could not control and felt it wiser to sell. I saw a great deal of opportunity for golf in China. Currently, it is the fastest growing golf industry in the world. There are more new golf courses under construction than anywhere else in the world. You will see many Chinese golfers come on and eventually dominate all world tours in the next ten years. I have a friend who is the head coach of the Chinese Olympic golf team. They have been training for the 2016 Olympics for two years.

Again, it is not in the best interest of my partners to share the current business I am involved except for Peter Sage. Had I not been injured I would have missed China. Do things happen for a reason?

DREAM BIG

After everything we've been through today as we read this book, I want to leave you with this: I DID IT. YOU CAN TOO!

As Napoleon Hill said in Think & Grow Rich, "Get going!" In the end, your success is my reward. Remember, if your goals and desires are stronger than the adversity that you face, and you will face adversity, then you will be successful. That is what will pull you through your brick walls. When you want something, when you want this business more than the aggravations that come up, as they come up, then you will get through those times and you will have the success you desire.

There really aren't any hidden secrets. What I have done, you can do too. The only real secret is to get going. In business, you must know that nothing begins until something is sold. You sell to your banker, to your clients, your family, and of course, you sell yourself on what you are doing. You must sell as a business person. The people who say they don't like selling aren't going to be good entrepreneurs. You need to sell yourself, your products, and your vision. The two biggest commodities that you have in your business are your time and your creativity. It's time for you to buy back your time so that you can get back to being creative, productive, and making money in your business.

If you're reading this book and you currently do not have a business, your first business will often serve as a training ground for you. For some of you who have a business and you need help, I can bring that help to you. What I have created, is two affiliate programs to help you get the training you need as well as have that training ground for your business so that you can also have your own success. The first one is my travel company **Wholesale Travel Passports** The second one is Entrepreneur Development Institute which gives you the ability to develop as an entrepreneur and be part of a group of people who are learning and developing together.

For more details, you can go to
www.ErrolAbramson.com
EntrepreneurialDevelopmentInstitute.com (USA)

EntrepreneurialDevelopmentInstitute.ca (Canada)
EntrepreneurialDevelopmentInstitute.co.uk (United Kingdom)

*If you are interested to bringing Errol to your country for
Speaking/Consulting, please message his team directly at
any of the websites mentioned above
Again, both of these affiliate programs are designed for you to start right now so you can get going and become the successful entrepreneur that you were meant to be.

I can tell you that it has been a rocky journey full of many emotional and physical ups and downs. There are no boundaries or obstructions that can keep you from your goals.

You must Dream Big because there is no magic in small dreams.

I did it, and I am still doing it and my friends - "YOU CAN TOO!"

Made in the USA
Columbia, SC
13 October 2018